This book is part of the Victor FAMILY CONCERN SERIES, a multivolume library dealing with the major questions confronting Christian families today. Each book is accompanied by a Leader's Guide for group study and a Personal Involvement Workbook for individual enrichment. All are written in a readable practical style by qualified, practicing professionals. Authors of the series are:

Anthony Florio, Ph.D., premarriage, marriage, and family counselor, *Two to Get Ready* (premarital preparation);

Rex Johnson, assistant professor of Christian education, Talbot Seminary, active in pastoral counseling, *At Home with Sex* (sex education and marriage preparation in the family);

Harold Myra, publisher of *Christianity Today, Love Notes to Jeanette* (sexuality and fulfillment in marriage);

J. Allan Petersen, speaker at Family Affair Seminars, *Conquering Family Stress* (facing family crises);

Nancy Potts, marriage and family counselor, *Loneliness: Living Between the Times* (dealing with personal loneliness);

Wayne Rickerson, family pastor, Beaverton Christian Church, Beaverton, Oregon and director of Creative Home Teaching Seminars, *Family Fun and Togetherness* (family togetherness activities);

Barbara Sroka, served on research and writing committees with Chicago's Circle Church and is active with their single adults, *One Is a Whole Number* (singles and the church);

James Thomason, assistant pastor at Calvary Baptist Church, Detroit, *Common Sense about Your Family Dollars* (family finances);

Ted Ward, Ph.D., professor and director of Values Development Education program at Michigan State University, *Values Begin at Home* (value development in the family);

H. Norman Wright, assistant professor of psychology at Biola College and marriage, family, and child counselor, *The Family that Listens* (parent-child communication).

Consulting editor for the series is J. Allan Petersen, president of Family Concern Inc.

GUIDE TO CURRICULUM SUBJECTS

	Wright—Communication THE FAMILY THAT LISTENS	Ward—Values Development VALUES BEGIN AT HOME	Thomason—Finances COMMON SENSE ABOUT YOUR FAMILY DOLLARS	Sroka—Singleness ONE IS A WHOLE NUMBER	Rickerson—Fun & Togetherness FAMILY FUN AND TOGETHERNESS	Potts—Loneliness LONELINESS: LIVING BETWEEN THE TIMES	Petersen—Crises CONQUERING FAMILY STRESS	Myra—Intimacy in Marriage LOVE NOTES TO JEANETTE	Johnson—Sex Education AT HOME WITH SEX	Florio—Premarriage TWO TO GET READY
adolescent children	*	*					*		*	
birth control								*	*	*
child development	*	*			*				*	
child discipline	*	*								
child communication	*	*			*		*		*	
church-family		*		*			*			
dating				*					*	*
death						*	*			
divorce				*		*	*	*		
emotions	*			*		*	*	*		*
engagement						*	*	*	*	*
finances			*				*			
friendship				*		*	*			
goals		*	*			*				*
leisure					*	*	*			
loneliness				*		*				

At Home With Sex

Rex Johnson

While this book is designed for the reader's personal enjoyment and profit, it is also intended for group study. A leader's guide is available from your local Christian bookstore or from the publisher at $2.95.

VICTOR BOOKS

a division of SP Publications, Inc., Wheaton, Illinois

Offices also in Fullerton, California • Whitby, Ontario, Canada • London, England

Scripture quotations are from the New American
Standard Bible (NASB), © 1960, 1962, 1963, 1968,
1971, 1972, 1973 by the Lockman Foundation, La
Habra, California. Used by permission.

Recommended Dewey Decimal Classification: 261.83418
    Suggested Subject Headings: SEX INSTRUCTION; FAMILY; FAMILY LIFE EDUCATION

Library of Congress Catalog Card Number: 79-65521
ISBN: 0-88207-639-6

VICTOR BOOKS
A division of SP Publications, Inc.
P.O. Box 1825 • Wheaton, Illinois 60187

CONTENTS

Foreword

North Americans like to think of themselves as sexually knowledgeable. When the time comes, however, for the average parent to educate his child in sexual procedures and meanings, he finds himself thrown into embarrassment and confusion and quickly finds something else to do.

Because many parents are so uneasy about discussing sex, their children grow through teenage to adulthood acquiring their sexual knowledge in school, and with friends, often in cars and at unchaperoned parties.

Because of the combination of ignorance, especially among our children, and embarrassment, especially among parents, we are offering *At Home with Sex* by Rex Johnson, as part of the Family Concern Series, with the hope that it will guide parents as they lead their children to an understanding of their sexuality.

The Family Concern series is an encyclopedia of practical family information prepared in response to the needs of contemporary families. It enables the church, with its unique built-in structures for education and enrichment, to meet these needs with a thorough and long-term plan. Pastors and church professionals will find in them an invaluable resource. They focus on the needs of singles, marrieds, parents and the family.

God uses people more than books to change people and, therefore, a unique feature of this series is that people work together on their family needs. Each book can be used in a group study for mutual learning, encouragement and support.

A Leader's Guide provides 13, one-hour, step-by-step study plans for adults in Sunday School, seminars, workshops, conferences, and retreats—complete with learning activities and visual aids.

The Personal Involvement Workbook enables each individual to get maximum benefit from the study whether alone, as a couple, or in a group. Worksheets and activity instructions are included. The chart on page 2 is a guide to the most important topics and where they are mentioned in each book in the entire series. It is a road map that will help you find quickly exactly the information you need.

A special word of thanks and appreciation goes to Norman Stolpe. As Family Concern's editorial director, he served as series editor for this project. His vision and relationship with the various authors enabled the concept to take form in reality. His hard work brought this series from planning to completion.

Victor Books and Family Concern have shared this vision and have cooperatively developed this comprehensive family ministry resource for individuals and churches. I trust God will deeply enrich your life and family through it.

J. ALLAN PETERSEN
Family Concern
Wheaton, Illinois

1

Sex Education—Who Needs It?

During a recent summer, I was a counselor at a high school camp. The kids were free to ask me any questions they wanted to, and I began to realize that there were a lot of questions that I wanted to hear that they weren't asking. Questions about the will of God, or getting along with parents, or loving each other. Questions like, "Why don't Christians give a rip about the thousands of people who are dying because of malnutrition?"

The kinds of questions I kept hearing were: "How far can we go on a date?" "Is oral sex OK for Christians?" "If someone in your family has forced you to make love, should you tell your fiance?"

I decided that the campers were only interested in one thing—sex. But then I realized that wasn't true. I needed to give them credit for being more than a bunch of erogenous zones. I still wonder if one of the reasons they were asking me was that they couldn't feel comfortable or safe asking their parents.

In a survey of 200 college students, 91 percent said their parents had given them no instruction about dating; 43 percent, no instruction whatsoever on sex; 82 percent, no warning about drinking, smoking, using drugs; 83 percent, no instruction at all about the use of money ("News for Thought," *Dads Only,* VI, No. 6, June 1978).

Moral Confusion

In 1977, *Time* Magazine commissioned the firm of Yankelovich, Skelly, and White to survey sexual morality. Among other things, they found that, though most Americans "are talking more openly about sex, they are increasingly confused about the moral values involved. While 68 percent agreed with the statement that 'it's a lot better to have openness about things like sex, homosexuality, premarital and extramarital relations,' 61 percent felt that 'it's getting harder and harder to know what's right and what's wrong these days.' Of these people, whom the Yankelovich survey categorized as 'morally confused,' the highest incidence occurred among those over 50 and, surprisingly, among those under 25" ("The New Morality," *Time* Magazine, Nov. 21, 1977, p. 112).

The Younger Set

Let's go a little younger than high school or college, to get in touch with the misinformation level.

● A Sunday School class of 13-year-old girls was discussing some of their sexual questions. The girls were embarrassed to say the word *intercourse* but referred to the act as "doing it" (Wilson W. Grant, M.D. *From Parent to Child about Sex,* Grand Rapids: Zondervan Publishing House, 1975, p. 18).

● One girl was told by her mother that saying the word *pregnant* was naughty. She was 12 years old before she learned that you could not become pregnant by holding hands, kissing, or by just saying "pregnant."

● Another girl wondered, "What's the belly button for?" When asked what *she* thought it was for, she replied that it was made by a big needle the doctor used to feed the baby after it was born. One of her friends had told her this. (Wilson W. Grant, M.D. *op. cit.*)

● "Sex must have something to do with sleep. My mother kept making me promise I would never sleep with anybody before I was married. And then she made me share my bedroom with my cousins when they came to visit."

● This is how a baby got into a tummy. You went to the doctor (with your husband) and told him you wanted one. Then you had to go to City Hall and fill out forms. Then God and the doctor and the city clerk picked out the right seed for you. The doctor told you how much to take and everything. Then you bought some big dresses and pulled down the shades. It took forever (Beatrice Braden, *Sex Was More Fun When,* Los Angeles: Price, Stern, Sloan, 1973).

Is there a need for sex ecucation? Let me tell you one more story, this time about an adult.

A young husband named Chris went to talk with a psychologist friend and ask for his help. Chris felt that his wife, Sally, no longer loved him because she was, as he put it, "shut up within herself." She behaved sharply with the children, was cross with him, and expressed bitter resentment.

Sally went to see the psychologist and as she talked about her life, he discovered that after her father died, when she was three, her mother had done all she could to protect Sally from the outside world by keeping her as close to herself as possible. One day when she was five, Sally and her mother stopped to look at a baby in a buggy on the street. "Where did that baby begin before it got into the buggy?" Her mother flushed and nervously pulled her away by the hand. "That's a question," she said, "nice little girls don't ask. When you get bigger, you'll learn about it."

Sally couldn't understand at the time what she had done to make her mother so cross, but she didn't want her to be like that again, so she didn't ask any more questions. There was something about babies and where they came from that made adults unhappy, she concluded. They didn't like to talk about it, so she wasn't going to stir up any unpleasantness.

As Sally grew older she learned more and more scattered bits of information about human reproduction from older girls, but always in an atmosphere of secrecy. This made her sure that her mother was right about the shamefulness of sex.

The end result of 20 years of a restrictive atmosphere was that when she married, Sally was not able to give or accept, fully and gladly, the physical expressions of married love. Her unconscious attitudes prevented the total surrender of herself. What began at the age of five, and developed through her entire childhood, became the root of her resentment and frigidity. It resulted in an unfulfilled marriage and an unhappy home. (Hugh C. Warner, "Puzzled Parents", as quoted in Erwin J. Kolb, *Parents Guide to Christian Conversation About Sex,* St. Louis: Concordia Publishing House, 1967, pp. 16-17).

Personal Values in Sex Education

Feeling that there was a distinct need for a book on sex education addressed to parents, I thought about my own approach in writing. For me such a book had to be personal. The only way I could write a book on sex education without it carrying my own values, opinions, viewpoints and biases would be to make it a physiological textbook. Even then my values would probably permeate it. But such textbooks are already available. So rather than trying to be neutral I will try to be explicit about my values and biases, inviting you to be aware of your own. If you find yourself disagreeing with me, that's all right. I hope I will help you in the education process as you teach your children from your own value structure.

The values I hold to are, first of all, *my* values. They are ideas, behaviors, and attitudes that I have invested in (bought) and so they are important to me. In other words, they are not the only "right" ways of thinking, behaving, responding, etc. I am in the constant process of examining my values in the light of Scripture. I hope you are too.

Thus, my values are subject to change, as I hope yours are. However, the more I've invested in an idea, behavior, or attitude, the harder it seems for me to relinquish it when I'm confronted with an alternative value. Since sexuality is an area of life that demands a lot of investment, change in sexual values comes rather slowly, if at all. Yet God calls us to change, to learn, in areas of high investment as well as in areas that don't mean much to us. I thank God that He is still working in me, even at the deep value levels, both to will and to do what He wants to do.

1. I value Christian marriage. According to Ephesians 5, it is one of God's pictures of how He relates to His people. I can better understand and live my relationship with God as I build and experience an intimate and loving relationship with my spouse. This includes my sexuality, as it is caught by and taught to my children.

2. I value sexual feelings and behaviors. They are a way of communicating love to my wife, and are a source of great pleasure and enjoyment to me. They are gifts from God for which I am thankful. They are the beginning of our children. They are a treasure to invest carefully, knowing that God will some day ask me about them. They are a part of my children's heritage—a heritage I must carefully pass on to them because I love them so much.

3. I value God's Word, the Bible. It is the one source of information about sex that comes directly from the Designer of sex. Without the Bible, "doing what comes naturally" eventually leads to distortion, corruption, and pollution.

4. I value my family. This means that I am learning to do whatever I can to make our lives meaningful, pleasurable, productive, and free. Sexually this means a growing intimacy with my wife, Eve, and preparation for fulfillment in love for my children.

5. I value the church—God's people. So I hope to enrich your life and the lives of your children by this written attempt to help you in the long and joyful ministry of sex education.

How Do People Learn?
Many people will probably never learn things such as the quantum theory of physics, the history of the Aymara Indians, or the process of second order factor analysis. But sexuality is so innate and important to human beings that they learn it one way or another. If parents can't or won't teach about sex, peers, teachers, books, or even the walls of public bathrooms fill the gap. That many young people get much of their sex education in the back seat of a car is a personal tragedy.

Anthropologist Louis J. Luzbetak points out that there are three distinct ways in which an individual learns:
- direct and conscious instruction called "education."
- deliberate observation and imitation.

• unconscious imitation and absorption. "This third manner of acquiring knowledge is perhaps more important than most people realize" (*The Church and Cultures,* Techny, Ill: Divine Word, 1963, p. 78).

Most people naturally think of sex education as *direct and conscious instruction.* Many parents then say, "Instruction is what schools are for. Sex education is the school's job. Besides, they have all the films and books. I don't." Teachers say that sex education is their job but that they are not the appropriate people to teach values, ethics, and morality. So they try to confine their education to the physiological and psychological aspects of sex education.

The trouble is that a school teacher's values and morality are communicated to his students implicitly even though he tries very hard to be neutral. They come out in his answers to questions, his attitude, and in nonverbal communication of his feelings. Few sex education teachers will have the same moral and ethical values that you want to communicate to your children. None of them can provide the setting of family love that parents can.

Some parents say that sex education is the church's job, especially where values and morality are concerned. But most churches say that sex education is the parents' job and that the church's job is to teach the Bible. So sex education, like a hot potato, is tossed around the circle, and the ones who get burned the most are the children and young people who aren't being taught. They get burned as they go elsewhere in their search for information.

But direct and conscious instruction is only a part of sex education. Much of a person's sexuality is learned by *deliberate observation and imitation.*

A boy, who has always seen his father treat his mother like a servant, will probably imitate his father's actions. He will also tend to talk and act this way toward other women and girls.

Little girls imitate their parents too, learning to be affectionate and responsive or learning to be defensive and unresponsive. By the time they are teenagers, some girls feel that sex is something you have to give a boy so he will love you. Many teenage boys in North

American culture think that it is part of being manly to try to go as far as possible on a date. "The girl is supposed to stop me if she doesn't want it."

Parents are not the only people children will imitate. Movie and TV actors, youth ministers, older brothers and sisters, and teachers are some possible sex models. But the influence of parents, especially on young children, is crucial for sex education. Most of the attitudes and values that cause sexual problems among young couples can be traced back to attitudes, behaviors, and values that were either consciously or unconsciously absorbed from parents.

The third kind of learning, *unconscious imitation and absorption,* is perhaps the most important. Children imitate the words, behaviors and patterns of their parents and others thereby picking up attitudes and feelings. But they also absorb attitudes, feelings, and values from their parents without being fully aware of it. One dad rarely reads, not even magazines or newspapers, but watches an average of three hours of TV a night. Another dad reads his own books and magazines, as well as reading to his children. Guess which ones will probably be more interested in school? Children whose parents respect and use literature are more likely to absorb this respect and interest.

Many children learn attitudes about sex from what their parents *don't* say. If parents don't initiate conversations about sex or if they give their children only partial answers (thereby often distorting the facts), their children have to figure one of two things: a. Sex is not important. This is obviously not true because of the tremendous place it has in advertising, because of the importance placed on it by peers, and because of the intensity of all those feelings that come with puberty. b. Sex is bad. Little children can absorb this idea and carry it right into adulthood. That God designed the human body for sex may be meaningful in theory, but not in the values by which they live.

Who and How?
The question is not whether or not sex education should take place. The questions are who will teach it, and how will it be taught.

Although sex education cannot be left to the school system alone, parents *can* be more creative in using the school as a resource for teaching. Schools often do have films and books to help parents. If parents show an interest in their children's education, most schools are happy to show parents the teaching aids they use, including books and films. These can be springboards for home and church discussions.

Sex education in church should supplement, not supplant, sex education at home. The family is a natural setting for discussions about sex. Information can be directly related to a child's or teenager's questions. Answers can be personal and specific rather than impersonal and general. The fear that peers will laugh if a child or teenager asks an embarrassing or a naive question is removed when sex education is a parental responsibility at home rather than a church responsibility. Your church can probably help you best by encouraging and preparing you to be your own children's teacher.

2

You Are the Teacher

Although you are probably convinced that you, as a parent, are the best one to teach your children about sexuality, you may have misgivings because you feel you do not know enough. Or you may be embarrassed to talk about sexuality with your children. Or perhaps you feel that you should have begun their sex education several years ago. Now they are teenagers and separate enough from you that it is going to be difficult. Or you may not even have children yet. Whatever your situation, part of this book, and maybe all of it, will be for you.

Attitudes

Before we can talk about sex education, we need to consider your attitudes. Children absorb their parents' attitudes. When your children become teenagers, they may question your opinions, but they will carry your attitudes into their own marriages. People absorb their attitudes, values, ideas, and behaviors in the area of sexuality from their total background. They also pass these on to their children, *even if they do not talk about them directly*. You already have an idea how much your children will imitate you and absorb your attitudes. Do you want them to catch your present attitudes concerning sex? Do you understand your own attitudes?

17

I'd like you to respond to a sex opinion questionnaire. You will not turn in your responses or send them to a computer for tabulation. In fact, you should write your responses on a separate sheet of paper, then after thinking them over and maybe discussing them with your spouse, burn the paper if you wish. Hopefully this questionnaire will be a mirror of your *attitudes* about sex even more than your opinions. Even if you have no children or are a single parent, you will profit by thinking through your sexual attitudes.

1. As an aspect of building and maintaining love in marriage, sex is:
   a. extremely important
   b. very important
   c. important
   d. relatively unimportant
   e. unimportant
   f. counterproductive.
2. For my spouse and me, sex is:
   a. a satisfying and delightful celebration
   b. something we look forward to
   c. a source of tension
   d. an obligation of marriage
   e. a routine.
3. The way my spouse reacts to me, I would say that he or she finds me:
   a. very attractive sexually
   b. attractive sexually
   c. sometimes attractive sexually
   d. sexually unattractive.
4. My spouse and I talk about sex:
   a. too much
   b. rarely
   c. often
   d. not enough
   e. freely.
5. How would I describe my parents' influence on me in the area of sexuality?

    a. They did not talk about sex.
    b. They taught me the "facts of life," but not the joy of sex.
    c. They adequately prepared me for my spouse.
    d. They taught me to thank God for sex.

6. The way I expect to influence my children in the area of sexuality is:

    a. to talk about it as little as possible
    b. to teach the "facts of life" but avoid the joy of sex
    c. to prepare them for their spouses
    d. to teach them to thank God for sex.

7. Sex education in our home is:

    a. uncomfortable—we have put it off until our children are older
    b. responsive—we respond carefully to our children's questions
    c. initiative—we initiate discussions periodically with our children.

8. If our children treat their future spouses as they observe my spouse and me treating each other, they will:

    a. experience a partnership of mutual support
    b. dominate or be dominated
    c. be distant and independent
    d. conflict regularly
    e. experience neither great problems nor great rewards.

9. Our children would conclude from our demonstrations of affection that our physical intimacies are:

    a. a source of joy
    b. a source of tension
    c. boring
    d. nonexistent
    e. mediocre
    f. embarrassing.

10. By observing their play and/or relationships with the opposite sex, I think our children:

    a. are looking forward to establishing their own marriages and families
    b. are indifferent to their future marriages and families
    c. would like to avoid establishing their own marriages and

 families
d. have not realized that they may have marriages and families in the future.

Now that you have completed the questionnaire, ask yourself one more question: Are you an "askable" parent? Your children's freedom to ask you questions about sex is their best protection from misinformation and unethical standards they may encounter from their friends, at school, in the media, and even at church. It is your monitor on what they know, what they need to know, and how their attitudes and values are developing. .

Coupled with their freedom to ask is your freedom to privacy. While you want to teach accurate information, positive attitudes, and biblical ethics, you also want to preserve the special atmosphere of mystery and awe about sex in marriage. In fact, much of your children's attitude toward sex and marriage will come from what they observe of your relationship. Is it attractive and desirable? Do your children see you and your spouse as a loving partnership? How well does your marriage represent God's intent for the total relationship of husband and wife?

Before we can say what sex in marriage should be, we need to define marriage itself. The following two sections are from the *Affirmation of the Family,* developed at the Continental Congress on the Family in St. Louis, in 1975.

The Origin and Purpose of Marriage

We believe that marriage was instituted by God at the beginning of the human race and was designed to involve the total, lifelong commitment of a man and woman to God and to each other. Therefore, marriage is an honorable status involving the privileges and responsibilities of mutual submission, companionship, respect, fidelity, sexual fulfillment, and procreation. It is a joyful joining of lives at many levels and provides the opportunity for mature love so vital to the wholeness of persons. (See Gen. 2:18-25; Ex. 20:14; Matt. 19:4-6; Eph. 5:21-33; 1 Cor. 7:1-5; 1 Peter 3:1-7.)

The Uniqueness of Christian Marriage

We affirm Christian marriage as a unique husband-wife relationship modeled after Christ's relationship to the church. In Christian marriage, the husband and wife strive to become one spiritually, intellectually, emotionally, and physically, and to function interdependently as equals in accordance with biblically prescribed roles. The husband is head of the wife. He is responsible to love her as Christ loved the church and as he loves himself.

The husband and wife dedicate themselves to the well-being of each other, cleaving, providing, and encouraging each other in their God-given freedom to develop their own gifts and abilities. The husband and wife are joint-heirs with Christ and share equally "in joy and in sorrow, in plenty and in want, in sickness and in health." The wife submits herself to her husband, loves him, and respects him. Christian marriage is meant to be a lifelong relationship between one man and one woman, indissoluble except by death. (See Matt. 19:3-12; 1 Cor. 7:10-15; Rom. 7:2-3; Eph. 5:21-33; 1 Peter 3:7; Prov. 31:10-31.)

Greater Sexual Intimacy

You can better understand and live your relationship with God as you build and experience an intimate loving relationship with your spouse. Conversely, a poor marital relationship is a poor picture of the way God relates to His people. One of the problems that usually accompanies a poor marital relationship is a low degree of sexual intimacy. This can be either a cause or result of the poor relationship. A low degree of sexual intimacy is one that either spouse considers inadequate.

An unsatisfactory level of sexual intimacy can be improved. New life can infuse a relationship that has gone stale. Enriching sexual intimacy in marriage can be the spark that ignites enriching changes in other areas of marital life.

One reason many parents find sex education with their children difficult is that they are not happy with their own sexual experiences as husband and wife. Maybe their expectations for sexuality were very high before they were married and their experience has given them the feeling that they are inadequate sexually. Maybe they feel embarrassed sexually or they get that feeling reflected from their spouses. In either case talking about sex with their children is very difficult.

If you have such a problem, the first step is to come to the place where you can talk freely about sexual topics with your spouse. Some couples find sexual intimacy difficult because they have not built intimacy in other areas of their life together as a couple. Most parents I know want to help their children to live the kind of life that will make them fulfilled, happy, and joyous as God's people. This includes giving them all the equipping that they need for sexual happiness in marriage. This is difficult unless the parents are building a sexually intimate and happy marriage themselves.

Building a happy sexual relationship in marriage is not something that is done before marriage, although premarital counseling can definitely help. Neither is sexual intimacy built on the honeymoon. It may get its start on the honeymoon, but sexual intimacy is something that must be built continually throughout the years of married life. It develops or deteriorates with the rest of a couple's relationship.

A sexual relationship cannot remain on level ground. It must be either developing or it begins to deteriorate by neglect. You may be happily married and sexually satisfied now, but you need to continue building and investing in your sexual intimacy for as long as you are together as husband and wife. Thus you will continue to grow and become a better teacher for your children.

Your Perspective on Sex

How do you view sex? Is it a concession that God made so that people could procreate? Is it equated with sin? Is it a dangerous tool or a powerful force in one's life? Is your attitude socioculturally or biblically conditioned? Are you squeezed into a sexual mold? Your perspective on sex will be one of the things that your children absorb from you. For Christian parents to have a basic biblical perspective on sex is important. Some basic assertions need to be made that will have a great deal to do with your perspective and how you train your children:

1. Sex is God's good gift to the people He created.
2. God designed sex to be part of a relationship of mutual commitment.
3. Sin distorts God's design for sex.
4. God forgives His people's sins, even sexual sins.
5. The indwelling Holy Spirit gives power to change.

God's Good Gift

The Bible asserts that God created sexual people "so God created man in His own image, in the image of God He created him; male and female He created them. . . . And God saw everything that He had made, and behold, it was very good" (Gen. 1:27, 31).

That sex is naturally pleasurable is a testimony to God's perfection as a designer and to His loving-kindness and consideration for His creation. "We have good news to proclaim about sex, and society needs to hear it. . . . Thank God for sex! The emphasis is on God because He is responsible for sex in the first place" (Harry Hollis, *Thank God for Sex,* Nashville: Broadman Press, 1975, pp. 14-15). *God designed the good gift of sex.* Sex, then, is not evil or even neutral; sex as God designed it is good. God not only made sex organs for people, but He also designed the use and function of those organs. Sex is God's chosen method for procreation, insuring the continuity of His crowning creation: humanity. God also intends sex to be the ultimate expression of and contributor to union in marriage.

To forget that God designed sex for people, whole people, is to separate one part of personhood for sexuality, leaving other parts for other kinds of interactions. In other words, sex becomes a role that can be played in or out of marriage. At this point lust becomes a problem.

Both physiologically and behaviorally, sex is a part of a whole person. Harry Hollis describes it as ". . . part of our total personalities. We do not have sex; we are sexual beings. Thus, a solely physical view of sex is contrary to biblical teachings. The body and soul are knit together in such a way that one is affected by the other. This unity of personhood stands against casual intercourse because the attempt to limit intercourse to physical involvement and pleasure violates the biblical teachings about the nature of human beings" (*A Christian Model for Sexual Understanding and Behavior,* Plenary Paper for the Continental Congress on the Family, St. Louis: Family 76, Inc., 1975, p. 5).

Relationships of Mutual Commitment

Mutual commitment is basic to God's design for sexual relationships. The mutual commitment of marriage is not only God's design for the beginning and the context of sexual expression; it is the culture in which sexuality develops in creativity and expressiveness. Growing mutual commitment is in turn the result of loving sexuality expressed creatively by whole people in a marriage relationship. The Bible portrays the marriage commitment as a covenant, parallel to other covenants in Scripture.

When whole persons interact with each other sexually as whole persons rather than as objects or fragmented, partial persons, their relationship is enhanced. Sexual intercourse adds unity, interdependence, pleasure, and communication to a total relationship. But when people interact with each other as objects, lust becomes a problem.

The commitment of marriage changes the character of lust to the wholesome natural desire for intimacy and sexuality as a component of the relationship. Two related Hebrew words sometimes translated "lust" clarify the nature of lust or desire within marriage.

Avah means "to desire," and is used in Deuteronomy 14:26 in God's instructions concerning tithing. When an Israelite could not take a tithe of his produce to the place God would choose, he was to convert his "first fruits" into cash and "spend the money for whatever your heart desires (*avah*), for oxen or sheep, or wine, or strong drink, or whatever your heart desires (*avah*)." What a surprise! God told His people they could buy whatever they lusted or desired, and with their tithe money, too.

The second Hebrew word, *avvah,* is used similarly in Deuteronomy 12:15, 20, and 21. Under certain conditions, within certain bounds, the Israelites could eat meat "in every desire (*avvah*) of your soul."

The point is that within God's design, desire—even strong desire—is not wrong; it is good. The Greek word, *epithumia,* illustrates this. According to W.E. Vine, it "denotes strong desire of any kind, the various kinds being frequently specified by some adjective" (*An Expository Dictionary of New Testament Words* Old Tappan, NJ: Fleming H. Revell, Co., 1940, Vol. 3, p. 25).

For instance, Jesus said, "I have earnestly desired (*epithumia*) to eat this Passover with you before I suffer" (Luke 22:15, NASB). Paul used the word in Philippians 1:23 NASB saying, "But I am hard pressed from both directions, having the desire (*epithumia*) to depart and be with Christ, for that is very much better."

Since marriage is God's design, strong desire within marriage is not only natural, but is blessed. Even anticipative desire that precedes marriage is natural and blessed! This is the overwhelming conclusion a person finds after even a cursory reading of the Song of Solomon. Further study of this book as Jody Dillow has done in *Solomon on Sex* (Nelson, 1977) substantiates this conclusion.

Sin Distorts Sex
Sexuality, like other areas of God's creation, is vulnerable to distortion by sin. Not that sex is sinful, but people misuse sex in sinful ways. Distortion is the result of the human attempt to redesign God's gift of sex. When used to conquer, to manipulate, to worship self or another person, or to demonstrate independence from God, God's gift of sex is redesigned to sin.

Distortion results in a solely physical view of sex. To compartmentalize body, soul, and spirit in one's self or another is to relegate sexuality to a purely physical function and sensuality to what Harry Hollis calls the "idolatry of pleasure" (*A Christian Model for Sexual Understanding and Behavior, p. 8).*

Distortion results in making people into sex objects instead of interacting as people in a total relationship. Devaluing people for one's own gratification is sin. This is evident in the negative use of the word *lust* in Scripture.

For example, Proverbs 6:25, NASB, speaking of an adulteress says, "Do not desire her beauty in your heart, nor let her catch you with her eyelids." The word "desire," sometimes translated "lust," is the Hebrew word *chamad*. Notice the object of desire is not a whole person, but her beauty. In this context, Socrates' comment, "Beauty is in the eye of the beholder," is noteworthy.

This is not to say that women should not be beautiful or make themselves attractive. The same word *chamad* is used in Genesis 2:9 to describe God's creation of trees as "pleasing to the sight." But trees are objects, not persons. To focus on people as sex objects rather than as sexual persons is to forget that God designed sex to be part of a relationship.

The Greek word *orexis,* translated "lust" in some versions, has the connotation of reaching or stretching after something. It is used in Romans 1:27, NASB, to describe people who abandoned heterosexuality and "burned in their desire towards one another." The picture is that of homosexuality in the context of using another person as a sex object irrespective of God's design for sex as part of a relationship.

Sex outside of the mutual commitment of marriage violates God's design, as revealed in Scripture, of mutual and loving sexuality within marriage. *Engaging in extramarital sex is sin.*

God Forgives
Fortunately, God is forgiving. *God forgives all sin for those who come to Him* asking for forgiveness, and this includes sexual sin! The realization that God forgives sexual sin can free a couple from guilt over their past. They can now enjoy new intimacy as they continue to establish their relationship with each other. This is because when they appreciate the forgiveness that God wants to give they can be released from the anxiety that comes because of sexual sin and causes them to seek release in other forms of sex exploitation.

Power to Change

With God's forgiveness comes the indwelling Holy Spirit who gives the power to live in ways that are different from one's former life. He gives the power to change behavior, including sexual behavior, if it needs to be changed. As He works, the fruit of His ministry becomes evident. This is described in Galatians 5:22-23 and is essential to growing sexual intimacy. If practiced in sexual intimacy, love, joy, peace, patience, kindness, goodness, faithfulness, gentleness, and self-control can help it to grow to new heights of joy and communicative love.

Statement on Human Sexuality

A statement on human sexuality was included in the *Affirmation on the Family* that was developed at the Continental Congress on the Family in St. Louis in 1975. I have quoted it to give you some idea of the range of concerns this includes and to prompt your further study.

The human body and the capacity for sexual relationship, enjoyment, and reproduction are God's gifts to be received in an attitude of thanksgiving, wonder, and joyful worship. We rejoice that God created male and female as sexual beings and we affirm that sexual intercouse within marriage is good, desirable, honorable, and consistent with personal holiness.

Parents are to convey such attitudes to children along with providing factual information. Parents and churches have a God-assigned responsibility to provide moral guidance by word and by example so that God's gift of sex will be used in ways honoring Jesus Christ.

We deplore distorted, unbiblical, and sinful sexual attitudes and practices, both within and outside marriage, which contribute to the breakdown of the family.

We resolve to resist the moral decline in our society, to teach that sex is to be enjoyed with mutual respect and fulfillment within marriage, and to proclaim that ultimate control results from Christian maturation, which is brought about by the power of the Holy Spirit through the fellowship of the faithful and through happy, useful service to Christ. (See Gen. 1:26-31; Deut. 5:18; 6:1-25; 1 Sam. 2:22; Ps. 139:13-18; Prov. 1:8-10; 5:18-19; 6:20; 7:27; 1 Cor. 6:14-20; 7:1-6; Eph. 6:4; 1 Thes. 4:1-8; 1 Tim. 4:3-5; Heb. 13:4.)

Further Exploration
Theologians and ethicists have given far more attention to these questions than I have here. Many important questions have been left untouched. What I have included is intended to help you receive and transmit to your children healthy sexual attitudes because you see sex in God's overall plan. If you wish to explore these issues further, the books listed in chapter 12 will be helpful.

3

A Family Atmosphere

It is so much easier to learn in some situations than in others. In one classroom, learning seems to be a joy while in another you can't wait for the hour to be finished. When I was in fourth grade in one school, I learned many things, but one thing that we didn't study was parts of speech. Then I attended fifth grade in another county, and found that all of my peers had already learned the parts of speech. I remember the day that my teacher discovered that I didn't know what nouns, verbs, adjectives, or adverbs were. She insisted that by the time I came back to school the next Monday I should have all of them learned. She showed me where the material was in the book, and I went home to learn the parts of speech in one weekend.

I appreciate my father for the time that he spent drilling me and explaining the tip-offs to tell which was an adjective or adverb. I came back to school the next Monday and passed the test. But to this day, my attitude about studying English grammar is not positive. In subsequent courses, whenever I had to study it, I found it difficult. Although I learned the parts of speech that weekend, I also acquired an attitude based on the pressured learning atmosphere.

Often the atmosphere in which people learn about sex is similar to the atmosphere in which I learned about the parts of speech. It is an atmosphere surrounded by fear and guilt, full of pressure and resulting in blame.

The Late Date Atmosphere

Two teenagers come home from a party, pull into the girl's driveway, park, and begin talking. They have been on several dates, and each time, since they started to express their feelings to each other physically, they have been going further and further. They may be focusing on physical feelings, but they are coping with pressures as well.

Some of these pressures are inward. Some they put on each other, and others are from their peers and the outside world. Most obvious is the *pressure to conform.* As teenagers talk with each other, they find out that there are some experiences that they have not had that other teenagers have. If a teen's friends are experienced in something that he or she is not, the pressure to conform to the expectations of one's peers is tremendous.

Second, is a *pressure to perform.* In the last several years, more and more open communication about sexuality has become the norm. The expectation that everybody can be a sexual superstar has evolved. Teenagers pick up this communication and expect to be masters of the sexual arts on their first or second try. But the back seat of the car doesn't lend itself to artistic sexual expression. A couple may fear getting caught, so they hurry. They are coping with feelings of guilt. One or both of them really may not want to be involved with the other sexually, but because of the pressure and expectation, they may submit anyway. Sex becomes something that a person does, in an atmosphere that is not conducive to the development of love, appreciation, and respect for another person.

Then there is *inward pressure,* especially on the adolescent boy. Physical pressure makes him conscious of his own feelings, of what is going on in his body, and very inconsiderate of what a girl is feeling. In the process of enjoying his own sexuality, he makes the whole experience rather miserable for her.

The result is that they have succeeded in having sex, but have missed out on what God intends it to be—a communication of love, respect, and trust between two people married to each other. They have also begun building an atmosphere for future sexual experiences which will make them much less than what God intends them to be.

The Honeymoon Atmosphere

Many people in Christian circles believe that the honeymoon is the best place to learn about sex. It is the best time to start experiencing sex, but the honeymoon can be charged with such tension, expectation, and pressure to perform, that it becomes a negative learning experience.

A couple who have not engaged in sexual expression prior to marriage now think they are supposed to be sexual experts. A couple who has had no premarital preparation can find their first experience of sex to be devastating. I am not suggesting premarital sex, but I do believe parents can help set an atmosphere for healthy, loving sex for their children's honeymoon. You can help make your children's honeymoons a more pleasant experience by giving them adequate premarital preparation.

Learning by Doing?

Educators point out that the best way to learn is through experience. So some parents have said, "We won't worry about sex education. We'll let our children experience sex once they are married. This will take some time and effort, but we wouldn't want to rob them of the joy of discovery."

But some kinds of sexual experiential learning can be very negative. Sex learned in the back seat of a car, in a cheap motel room, or even on a honeymoon—without the building of a healthy atmosphere for sexuality—is likely to be negative and repulsive rather than positive and enjoyable.

Society pays close attention to atmosphere in most areas of life. For instance some restaurants are built around an atmosphere. Their food may be average or even rather poor and tasteless, but if they have built a good atmosphere, people will come to eat and enjoy their time there anyway. Even fast food chains carefully choose their colors, waitresses, menus, the pictures on the wall, the neighborhood in which they attract people on the basis of atmosphere.

An atmosphere for the learning of sexuality needs to go beyond thinking about the kind of atmosphere in which the couple is going to have their first sexual experience. I believe the best place to learn sexual attitudes is in a particular kind of family atmosphere. You can create an atmosphere in your family for your children that will enable them to understand sex, avoid many of the problems of those who have been misinformed, and make their first experiences with sex a joy rather than a guilt-and-fear experience.

Five Common Family Atmospheres

1. Personal exploitation. Many children today are introduced to sex by their parents. *Newsweek* Magazine, November 10, 1977 estimates that 150,000 children are sexually molested annually, most of these by their parents or stepparents. The American Humane Children's Division estimates sexual child abuse is three times as common as child battery. What a terrible way to learn about sex.

2. Taboo. A much more common family atmosphere concerning sexuality is taboo. In many Christian homes sex is a taboo subject not to be talked about or mentioned. Parents may be so uncomfortable with their own sexuality that whenever sex comes up as a topic of conversation, it is quickly squelched. Children learn it is wrong to ask questions about sex or about bodily functions that have to do with elimination or reproduction. They discover that curiosity about other people's bodies and the opposite sex will not be answered at home. They have picked up the attitude that the parts of their body that have to do with reproduction are dirty.

3. Pass the buck. Some families practice the family atmosphere of *taboo,* even though they may not consciously avoid talking about sex. The family that passes the buck when it comes to sexual conversation is a family that is probably not comfortable with the subject. Sex education is left to the school, the church, or the neighborhood. Maybe these parents feel inadequate when talking about sexual matters or just embarrassed, but children learn that they cannot come to Mom and Dad and ask questions. They have to get their answers elsewhere. They may get information from good, healthy authoritative sources or they may get it from peers or the media. In the process they can learn stereotypes and misinformation.

4. Procrastinating families. Some parents intend to tell their children about sex but they keep putting it off, waiting until the children are mature enough to hear about the "birds and the bees." They estimate an age at which it is proper for their children to learn about sex and they wait until that age comes. If they are uncomfortable about their own sexuality, they keep putting off the discussion—which is somehow going to be a magical introduction to sex. They act as if the child has existed without sexuality from the beginning and now is going to be introduced to the whole subject in one conversation. Somehow this conversation is going to keep him from ever having problems again. Very often procrastinating families continue procrastinating until long after their children have learned much about sex from their peers, bathroom walls, or other adults.

5. Speaking the truth in love. The context of Ephesians 4:15 does not deal with sex education, but with learning in the family of God. I think it can apply to sex education as well. It says "But speaking the truth in love, we are to grow up in all aspects into Him, who is the head, even Christ." Parents can build an atmosphere in which it is natural to speak the truth in love, even when subjects come up that would tend to embarrass someone in the family.

Sex is certainly not a taboo subject in the Bible. The Old Testament Law included judgments about seduction, bestiality, homosexuality, incest, adultery, and rape. The whole Book of Hosea is a picture of God's relationship to Israel as she plays the harlot and breaks her covenant with God. Second Samuel 11—12 describe in detail David and Bathsheba's adulterous relationship; 2 Samuel 13 describes Amnon and Tamar's incestuous relationship. Jesus spoke about adultery and lust in Matthew 5:27-28. In

Romans 1:19-27, Paul named sexual deviations and in 1 Corinthians 6:9, 10, 13-20, he talked about adultery.

Many passages in Scripture refer to sex and the family on a more positive tone—such as the Song of Solomon, the love poem of a bride and groom. Or the instructions Paul wrote to first-century Christians about marriage. The Scripture gives us an example to approach this subject with frankness and love which seeks the best.

In Love

"Speaking the truth in love" starts with parents who are so obviously in love with each other that their children can absorb and imitate their interactions with each other. Boys learn how to treat girls by watching how Daddy treats Mommy. Girls learn how to relate to boys by watching how Mommy relates and responds to Daddy. So parents who love each other provide for their children a model for healthy relationships between a husband and wife. Some parents love each other but do not communicate that love except when they are by themselves. This really does not help their children.

Children need to see love communicated in conversation and in practice so that they can learn to communicate love too. I'm certainly not suggesting that the parents should invite their children to watch them make love sexually. I am saying that husbands who respect their wives and love them openly, who are affectionate and demonstrative in their love, will encourage their children to be affectionate and demonstrative in their love too, and will help them learn to express it.

Parents who love their children will want to do everything they can to make their experiences with sex joyful and meaningful. Children's attitudes about sex are largely determined by how their parents live, think, and interact with each other and how they answer questions. Parents may have to wrestle with their own feelings about sexuality—because they love their children. They may be comfortable in their relationship with husband or wife, but not in talking about it with their children.

But because parents love their children, they will go beyond that embarrassment to the point of being able to discuss sexuality freely. Parents who love their children will develop an atmosphere of openness in communication about relationships. It takes time and energy to work and play together, to search and discover together, and just to live as a family. Time together gives children the freedom to open up and ask questions from their own curiosity.

Speaking the truth in love also implies love for your children's friends. No matter how careful a parent is in his sex education program, his children will pick up terms and ideas from their friends. Parents can react negatively and defensively, or they can choose to love their children's friends. This may mean accepting a child, even though his language is foul. It will probably mean explaining words and ideas that your children hear from friends. It will certainly mean helping your children discover their values, and their responses to sexuality as portrayed in our society. Love is basic to speaking the truth because without love, children will not trust their parents enough to be honest with them.

The Truth
If children believe babies are brought by storks or purchased at stores, it is because their parents told them this or failed to correct this impression. When they realize that they have been misinformed, their feelings of trust for their parents may turn to disillusionment.

Another area where many parents have problems is in accurately naming the parts of the body. Parents who have difficulty using the words *penis* and *vagina* communicate to their children that something is wrong with these words and, maybe, wrong with the parts of the body.

Speaking
Speaking the truth in love requires communication. The attitude that you can talk about anything in your family is the kind of open atmosphere in which you provide quality sex education. Parents can build this kind of attitude by being honest in answering questions which might be embarrassing. Curiosity about sex is natural

for children of all ages. Sometimes they ask questions just at the wrong time, like when your mother-in-law is visiting, or when you're standing and talking to your pastor. It is perfectly acceptable to say, "Son, I'll respond to your question later. Right now I want to continue my conversation with Grandpa." Then be sure you do come back later and answer the question.

You also need to initiate conversations about sex and sexuality. Sometimes children don't know what questions to ask. Sometimes their attitudes about sex have been formed by their interactions with peers and a new perspective needs to be given. You can create a healthy, open atmosphere for family communication about sex by periodically investing time in initiated conversations about sexuality with your children.

Much sex education will be on a one-to-one basis, father-son, father-daughter, mother-son, mother-daughter. But sometimes family communication needs to take place. If your family can really talk about anything in an open and honest atmosphere, children will learn attitudes that are positive and joyful about their sexuality.

Sex is generally not considered a dinnertime conversation topic, but for some families that is the only time they are together to talk. So maybe it would be a good topic for some dinner conversations. Sex is not generally considered a topic for devotions, but maybe family devotions ought to center periodically around sexuality. After all, it was God who invented it. Other times for family discussion about sex might be after watching a TV show or a movie, or after reading an article in the newspaper or a Scripture passage that talks about sexuality.

The goal is to give your children the freedom to communicate with you about their feelings and attitudes as they develop in their sexuality. To reach that goal you need to be comfortable with your own sexuality. If you are not, you can talk first with each other, as husband and wife, to help you become more comfortable in talking about sexual matters with your children.

In summary, the atmosphere that you create for learning about sexuality in your family is crucial to the development of healthy attitudes and behaviors in the next generation of your family. You can allow poor atmospheres to prevail, or you can decide to develop a healthy atmosphere in your family. You can conform to society's roles and expectations, developing an atmosphere of personal exploitation or taboo, passing the buck, or procrastinating. Or as Christian parents you can speak the truth in love about sexuality. If you do, your children will grow in maturity and appreciation for you. And the communication of love and sex within your marriage is likely to grow.

Truth is specific. We need to be accurate in the words we choose and the descriptions we give. We should be able to talk about any aspect of sexuality—either as it arises or as we initiate conversations about it.

Perfection is not required in sex education. You educate your children in many ways in which you don't tell them everything perfectly. You may teach your children to drive, but you don't ask them to become race drivers. You teach them to handle money, but you don't require them to become accountants. Don't feel that you must be perfect in your sex education either. You will make mistakes. At times you won't be able to conceal your embarrassment. In some areas you may not be able to be totally honest. But don't give up and develop taboo subjects, pass the buck, or procrastinate. Love your children even when love is uncomfortable.

4

Response—Ability

Lisa was a ninth-grader, blonde, blue-eyed, petite, and friendly. She seemed smart enough to do anything she wanted to. Yet her grades were below average. She grew up in a solid middle-class home with her parents and two brothers. Her friends saw her as a follower rather than a leader. She went to church with her parents and was involved in the youth group. She was also involved at school in a couple of clubs and had aspirations of being one of the school's cheerleaders.

Two months into the school year, she started dating Tom. He was a junior, on the football team, and admired by most of the kids in the school. Before long, their frequent dates were taking them later and later into the evening, and they were spending more and more time parked in her driveway, "talking" in his car.

Then Lisa's parents began to notice a change in her attitude. She became anxious, did not talk with them much, and seemed to avoid eye contact with them. Her mother asked her, on different occasions, what was bothering her. Her answers were always something like, "Oh, nothing that I can't handle." Then she would change the subject and leave the room. Finally one evening, as Lisa's mother walked by her daughter's closed bedroom door, she thought she heard her sobbing, so she knocked and went on in.

Lisa began pouring out her story between sobs. She told how she had gotten more and more intimate with Tom and how eventually their petting and necking had led to having sex, "getting it on" in her words. Then she found out she was pregnant. This worried her to the point that she was sick, couldn't eat, and felt that she needed to run away from home. Tom suggested to her that everything could be taken care of if she had an abortion. The idea seemed like a way of escaping all the worry that was making her sick. So she went ahead with the abortion.

Now she was all mixed-up because she felt terribly guilty about what she had done. Not only that, she thought that she still loved Tom but she wasn't sure if he loved her anymore. She knew that by sharing her story with her mother she would be dragging her family into her problems, but she couldn't face it on her own any more.

Roots of Responsibility

Lisa's story is not unusual. The National Institute of Health reports that in the last several years sexual activity among women aged 15-19 has increased 30 percent in the United States. Over half of these teenagers have had intercourse, and though many use oral contraceptives or IUDs, few use contraceptives when they first begin intercourse. Many wait until pregnancy occurs. When a family finds itself in the midst of the heartache and stress that result from premarital pregnancy and abortion, the parents often ask, "Why did this happen to us?" and "How could this be?"

To trace every answer back to one situation or reason would be oversimplifying, and beside the point. The question may be best approached from a perspective of a family that has not yet had to face the issue of premarital pregnancy or abortion. For them it is phrased, "How can such a scene be prevented?" Is there a way of reducing the likelihood of premarital sex, pregnancy, and abortion?

While there are no guarantees, parents can reduce the likelihood of such traumas if they begin to teach their children responsibility when they are very young. Many teenagers get into sexual trouble because they have not learned responsibility. They have not had to face the consequences of their behaviors, because parents are there to take responsibility. Therefore, when negative consequences are predicted for premarital sexual activity, they cannot understand the gravity of the warning. Nor do they understand the painful problems in which they will find themselves if they violate God's laws concerning relationships, particularly in the area of sexuality.

Learning responsibility goes hand in hand with valuing. They will tend to hold in higher value things for which they have responsibility. Because many teenagers have not learned to value anything very much, they do not value their bodies or their personalities significantly enough to hold them back from sexual promiscuity. Certainly if a teenager doesn't value himself he will not value the body or personality of another. In an age when contraception and abortion are readily available, many teenage boys take no responsibility for the consequences of sexual activity.

To expect a great amount of responsibility from a teenager in a hedonistic society may seem unfair, especially if his parents have not demonstrated responsibility. The clouding of standards for right and wrong behavior puts considerable pressure on young people to make decisions about their conduct. When their elders cannot even decide what is right or wrong, teenagers have little to guide them.

But Christians have a very clear standard of right and wrong, given to us in the Scriptures. As Christian parents demonstrate and verbalize the standards that are in the Bible, their children can learn to understand their responsibilities in sexual conduct, as well as in other areas of life.

In Joshua's last speech to the nation of Israel before he died, he issued a challenge which is relevant today. "And if it is disagreeable in your sight to serve the Lord, choose for yourselves today whom you will serve; whether the gods which your fathers served which were beyond the river, or the gods of the Amorites in whose land you are living; but as for me and my house, we will serve the Lord" (Josh. 24:15, NASB). A choice to serve the Lord includes a responsibility to understand His will and obey it. This may mean a conflict between what society condones and God's standard.

Even a cursory reading of Scripture shows that God considers adultery sinful and wrong. In sex education, God's people must teach their children a biblical standard. Yet, conscientious Christian parents have been teaching a Christian standard for years, and some of their teenagers have still gotten into trouble sexually. What went wrong? One answer might be that while these teenagers were aware of the biblical standards for morality, they did not assume responsibility for living moral lives before God. If a teenager is sexually responsible, it is because he learned responsibility as a child. Thus, teaching responsibility is a part of sex education and it needs to start when a child is very young.

Response-Ability

When faced with temptation or any other choice, for that matter, the question of responsibility comes in. A common excuse after something has gone wrong is, "Well, I didn't have any choice." Only rarely is this true. One way to define responsibility is the ability to respond appropriately to stimuli that come our way. Or we could say that in the choices available to us, a responsible person consistently decides for the better options. One way of learning responsibility then, is to have to face consequences. For instance, when a child never deals with the consequences of his behavior because his parents do it for him, he has a difficult time learning new ways of responding. He will continue to respond in all the old ways that have been successful for him even though they are disruptive for others.

Our son, Matthew, is learning the responsibility of taking care of his room and doing his chores in the morning before going to school. His mother or I can hover over him and make sure that all this is taken care of, or we can let him face the consequences of not having it done when it is time to leave. If this happens, he has to face a teacher who will put him through some stress for arriving late. He is beginning to learn that he has plenty of time to get up, make his bed, dress, fix up his room, and take out the trash. Then he can eat breakfast and have an hour to play before going to school. Hopefully we are teaching him the responsibility of doing what has to be done before taking time for the pleasurable things he wants to do.

A second way to learn responsibility is for parents and children to talk through the different options available before a particular problem comes up. For instance, Matthew has not had to face the temptation to use drugs. Although older children are dealing in drugs at his school, they have not bothered the first-graders yet. But we have discussed and we will continue to discuss his options when somebody tries to induce him to experiment with drugs. We want him to have previously considered his options so that he will be able to predict the consequences of each before he has to make his choices. Without this forethought, he would face the pressures of his peers without any reasons for saying No.

For instance, if a mother has not talked with her daughter about the girl's options when she is in a car alone with a boy, that girl may face a situation that she cannot deal with. She has not thought through the consequences of saying Yes to a boyfriend, or at what point in their intimacy she is going to draw the line and stop his sexual advances.   If, however, she and her mother have talked through the options, she at least has more choices available, more of a sense of personal power, and she can resist persuasion much more easily.

A negative aspect related to responsiblity is manipulation. Sometimes parents want so badly for their children to walk in a certain way that they take choices away so that their son or daughter will only have one choice. For instance, a teenage girl brings home a new boyfriend and introduces him to her father. He strikes the father as not being the kind of boy that he wants his daughter to date. Maybe through his conversation, behavior, and demeanor, he communicates selfishness.

Because this dad loves his daughter and does not want her hurt, he may begin to think how he can keep her from dating this boy. At this point whatever he does to meet that objective could be called manipulation. Maybe he grounds his daughter for two or three weeks. Maybe he lectures her. Maybe he tries to arrange a date with another boy he thinks is more acceptable (the matching game).

Jesus' parable in Luke 15 is an interesting comment on manipulation. The young son said to his father, "Give me the share of the estate that falls to me." So the father, rather than manipulating his impulsive son, gave him his share of the estate. Not long after that, the boy took everything he had and left. Notice that the father, who is a model of God, let him go. Not only that, but he did not chase after him and try to get him back. The younger son went to a faraway country and squandered all of his estate with loose living. Eventually he got into a financial depression and was in physical need so desperate that he put himself into the service of a citizen of that country who sent him into the field to feed the pigs. In fact, he was so hungry that he was to the point of competing with the pigs for their food.

When he finally came to his senses (an interesting study in itself), and realized that he would be much better off if he were hired by his father, he started back home. While he was still a long way off, his father came to meet him. He reestablished this rebel to the position of sonship instead of slavery or even employment, and had a feast for him. This father did not manipulate his son but allowed him choices that led to natural consequences in which he would learn about life.

All the sex education you may give your children cannot guarantee a failure-proof life sexually. You can't insure that they won't be promiscuous before marriage, or after. But as you teach your children responsibility, you can lower the probability that they will act irresponsibly as teenagers and young adults. They will know that the choices they make have a tremendous bearing on their future.

Norm Wright, in a cassette series titled "Sex and the Bible" explains a chart that shows different options for intimacy for a couple as they approach and go on into marriage. Talking through this kind of chart together as your children start dating, would be an excellent experience in preparing them for the responsibilities of dating.

Another responsibility-building tool, described in Norm Wright's book *Communications—Key to Your Teens,* is a covenant or an agreement between parents and teenagers about important aspects of responsibility. Parents and teenagers may make a covenant about dating, or driving, or other areas of life. Covenants convert unspoken agreements into speech and writing. They tend to lessen misunderstanding and clarify the expectations that parents and teenagers have of one another. They are helpful in building responsibility. Covenants do not have to be limited to teenage years. In fact, short concise covenants can be made with even younger children.

Learning Responsibility from the Start

One of the first developmental tasks of babies, toddlers, and little children is learning to trust, and to be trusted. Being trusted is next to impossible if a person has not first learned to trust. Trustworthiness is something that is built on the basis of trust relationships and a child needs to experience trust in his parents or other people before he will become trustworthy himself. So one of the first elements in responsibility-building is for parents to be very careful with the trust that children have in them.

In the very early years, physical affection is important for building trust. When small children wrestle with Daddy, trust is built because they know that someone who could very easily hurt them doesn't because he loves them. They trust him to throw them in the air and catch them. They can trust Mommy to love them and take care of them when they need her too. When trust is broken in early childhood it is very difficult to rekindle it. People who have not learned to trust have a very difficult time assuming adult responsibilities.

Part of childhood trust is being confident in parents' promises. Promises are to be kept, and this is sometimes difficult for parents of young children, because they keep asking for things. Parents are so eager to give their children the experiences and objects they ask for that they often promise more than they can possibly perform. To promise less and do more would be better for teaching responsibility.

Nobody is perfect, but a consistent record in promises kept is very important. Many times I have promised my children to take them to the park, and we have not gotten there. Sometimes this is because I haven't made keeping my promises a high enough priority. Other times something they wanted to do more than going to the park changed the promise. But as much as possible, if we are not going to be able to keep our promises, we try to get the children's permission to postpone the activity. Usually this involves letting them know when we intend to keep the promise we made. We are learning not to make a promise when we are not absolutely sure we can keep it. Maybe that means saying, "I can't promise you that toy, that experience, or that trip, but we would like to and will do it if we can."

Another behavior that little children can begin learning is accountability. This means that they are periodically responsible for various tasks. The chores already mentioned would be one example of accountability. Our children know that we will be checking to see whether or not their rooms are cleaned. Little children cannot be held accountable for everything they do, but they should begin to be accountable for some specific responsibilities or behaviors. Very young children start with just one or two behaviors. Then as they grow into their threes, fours, and fives, you can add behaviors for which they will be accountable.

It helps children become accountable when their parents volunteer accountability for their behavior. Again this is not accountability for all of life; rather, parents can choose one behavior for which they would like to become accountable to their children. Then they ask their children to hold them to it. If parents model the volunteering of accountability when their children are young, the children, as they grow, will find reciprocating easy. Then discipline does not have to be coercive.

Skills and Autonomy

As children grow toward school age, they concentrate more and more on the development of various skills. They also become more autonomous during these years, sensing themselves as separate from their parents and from other people. Along with autonomy comes responsibility. So parents can help build responsibility in their school-age children by encouraging them, first by building pride in their achievements.

Children at this age are very achievement-oriented. Parents may be able to draw, sing, play an instrument, shoot a basket, or throw a football much better than their children. But building pride in children's achievements is a crucial aspect of building responsibility. So keep encouraging them.

Second, parents help them learn responsibility by making them more responsible for their own possessions. The care they take of their toys, their schoolwork, their pets and other possessions, becomes a very good evaluating device for parents.

Because a child at this age is learning autonomy, parents must do everything they can to build a strong self-image in the child. Children and teenagers with a strong self-image are generally able to make responsible choices. They also find it easier to say No to peer pressure. This kind of responsibility is taught over many years, slowly and carefully.

"The way of a fool is right in his own eyes, but a wise man is he who listens to counsel" (Prov. 12:15, NASB). Finding and choosing wise counsel is an aspect of growing up that strengthens responsibility in children and teenagers. It does run counter to their autonomy, to their feeling that they have to prove they are right. But part of real wisdom is getting wise counsel. Parents who model the search for wise counsel encourage their children to seek and gain wise advice. When older children have sought and listened to wise opinions, parents can often affirm and reinforce them even if they don't fully agree with their decision.

Identity and Values

In the teenage years, a person's own identity develops and his values become life-changing and life-directing values. This is not to say that teenagers reject the values their parents have taught them over the years they have been together. It is to recognize that during the teenage years, the family's values are often questioned. To give children the rationale behind your values is critically important.

Part of the process of learning one's identity and restructuring one's values is the gaining of emotional independence. At the same time a teenager is focusing on independence, his parents are wanting him to learn self-discipline.

Parents think that if a teenager proves that he is self-disciplined enough to regulate his behavior, he has proven that he can be given independence. Teenagers think that self-discipline is not the issue. They believe that they can prove themselves disciplined once they are given independence enough to prove their self-discipline and maturity.

This tension is a very natural aspect of growing up. Rebelling and learning independence are not the same thing although sometimes rebellion is an aspect of learning independence, if the child has not been given sufficient responsibility for choices and behavior.

Parents can build a climate for teenagers to learn self-discipline along with independence, and grow toward responsibility. Parents can create a climate for this learning by encouraging personal exploration and discovery; encouraging individual differences so that teenagers feel free to be themselves and express themselves; accepting mistakes as well as excellence; tolerating ambiguity so that teenagers can respond to conflict without immobilization.

The teenage years are full of competition, and the home cooperation and collaboration are important. Teenagers tend not to be open if they feel the need to be perfect. Parents can encourage personal vulnerability. If parents allow teenagers to know that their parents are not people who "have it all together" but are "getting it together," then teenagers can be happy to get it together too. Parents can encourage acceptance of other people and of themselves. God accepts us just as we are when we come to Him, and teenagers need to learn to be accepted as well. Parents can encourage respect, both self-respect and respect for others.

In summary, one of the crucial aspects of sex education for Christian parents is that of teaching children responsibility. It is a long, slow learning process with many setbacks. Sometimes responsible children and teenagers are irresponsible. Sometimes irresponsible children and teenagers are responsible. The question is, *As*

your children grow are they becoming more and more responsible?
If they are, they are more likely to be ready for the kinds of choices
that will confront them when they are teenagers.

5

Communication in Sex Education

We have considered attitudes, atmosphere, and responsibility. You may be asking, "When do we get down to talking? In the final analysis, sex education comes down to what I *say* when my son or daughter asks a question about sex." Natural conversation is probably the easiest way to approach sex education. Sometimes parent-child conversations turn out to be lectures by parents to children. Having a good conversation about sex with a child or teenager is something of an art. There are four things you can do to make sure you have a teaching conversation and not a lecture or strained silence.

Accept Your Child's Feelings
A child's feelings are sometimes threatening to parents. Curiosity about a subject with which parents are uncomfortable or uninformed elicits feelings of discomfort. When parents sense that their children do not trust them as they used to, or do not love them in the way the parents wish for, they can feel threatened. Many parents find it difficult to accept feelings of unhappiness or sorrow in their children because they love them and want them to be happy and joyful. So when a child is perplexed, confused, frightened, or sad, parents sometimes deny their children those feelings. They

may say, "Oh, it will be all right. You can quit crying now."

Another source of threat for parents is a teenager's first boyfriend or girlfriend. This is intensified if the parents do not approve of the friend. However if the parents value communication with their children, it is necessary that they accept their children's feelings, even if they don't agree with the ideas behind them.

Accepting children's feelings calls for the ability to notice how your children react to what you say and let them know that you sense their reaction. For instance, you might say something like, "You seem to be upset by what I'm saying." Or, "You find that idea amusing, don't you?" "That sounds a little funny, doesn't it?" "That threatens you?" "What do you think about that?" These are meant to elicit a child's honest description of what he is feeling.

Accepting your children's feelings is important, even when they are negative. This will help them to relax and have confidence that you love them, accept them, and don't have a need to change them. Children want their parents' approval. Right up into the junior high years, approval is so important that children will look for the answer that they think parents want rather than the truth. So if negative feelings are unacceptable to their parents, they will conceal or lie so as not to incur the disapproval of their parents.

If negative feelings are going to be changed, they need to be talked about, not hidden or concealed. Sometimes a child's feelings are in direct opposition to Scripture. For instance, what if a child expresses feelings of hate for somebody? Scripture says that we are to love even our enemies. Or what if a teenager expresses feelings of lust when he has been in the presence of a girl? When confronted with feelings that they don't like, children have four basic choices.

1. They can deny or repress them. Children are taught to repress their feelings by parents, teachers, and peers who will not let them talk about what they feel. For instance, when a four-year-old girl walks into the living room with only her panties on, she is surprised to see some of her parents' friends. Her mother is embarrassed because her daughter does not have all her clothes on and tells her loudly, and with embarrassment, to run back into her room and put her clothes back on, right away.

The child begins to sense that something about her body is shameful. Her mother's friends cannot see her this way! When she is a little older and has a slumber party, the subject of sex comes up. The girls are naturally curious and want to know about each other. As they talk, the girl's mother walks in and hears a bit of the conversation. If she bawls them all out for talking about "things that they shouldn't be," this girl may repress some more.

As part of her preparation for junior high school, the girl's mother takes her aside and lectures her for an hour about "the birds and the bees." She may tell her daughter that she is not to talk about sex with other people but that she needs to know some facts before she goes to junior high.

As she enters puberty, this girl begins to feel new things about herself and about boys. But she is afraid to talk about her feelings with anyone. Her mother has already warned her that these are things that people don't talk about. So she continues to repress.

When she starts dating, she finds herself in a dilemma, because she cannot deny some very strong feelings. Maybe her boyfriend tells her that he loves her and wants to prove his love to her. He begins kissing and hugging her, and she continues to sense feelings that she has not been able to talk about. Obviously she cannot talk about them with her boyfriend. For teenagers in this circumstance to understand the differences between love and infatuation, between their feelings of sexual desire and needs for love and affection, is impossible.

Later still, if she becomes a bride, she finds that she has another problem. Now she is supposed to be intimate, open, and free about her body and her husband's body. This is totally against everything that she has been taught to do for many years. By now she may have learned enough to understand that in marriage everything about sex is God-given and good. Maybe she understands sexuality in terms of "how to make her husband happy." Her *ideas* about sex may have even changed to positive ideas. But her *feelings,* when she is involved in sexual activities, are different from her ideas. As much as she would like to feel that sex is wonderful, God-given, and intimate, she somehow feels an aspect of dirtiness, immorality, and wrong. Repression of feelings about sexuality is not a good alternative.

2. *They can express their feelings.* Unfettered expression of sexuality would mean acting out all of the sexual feelings that a person has. Some people advocate such unrestrained expression. But God put full expression into the context of marriage. Only within marriage is this acceptable. So obviously a child needs a better alternative than free expression.

3. *They can suppress their feelings.* Suppression is the conscious inhibition of sexual feelings and is often quite appropriate. For instance, if a teenage boy becomes sexually aroused when a classmate walks into the room, he is not going to then make sexual advances to her. He continues to sit at his desk, maybe thinking about her or admiring her, but realizing that if he expressed his feelings he would be socially ostracized and punished by school authorities. The consequences are bad enough that he consciously inhibits his feelings.

An adult might become quite sexually aroused at the dinner table. For him to take his wife into their bedroom, lock the door, and express his love to her intimately would be appropriate to their relationship, but not to their plans for the evening. The family is eating dinner and some friends are coming over later. So he suppresses his feelings until after the company has left, and he and his wife go off to bed.

4. *They can admit or confess their feelings.* By confession I mean talking to God and to a significant other person. Openly admitting feelings helps a person deal with them in appropriate ways. If children learn through experience with their parents that talking about their feelings is acceptable—even negative and threatening feelings—they can establish a pattern of dealing with their feelings on a regular basis. In conversations about sexuality, this means that parents will avoid statements like, "You shouldn't feel that way about her." "Don't say that!" Statements such as these will work better: "You sound quite attracted to her." "Does talking about these feelings threaten you?" "Tell me how you feel about it."

Accept Your Children's Ideas

A second way to help stimulate conversation with your children about sexuality, as well as about other areas of interest, is to accept their ideas. Accepting ideas with which you agree is easy, but it's more difficult to be accepting when you disagree. Accepting and agreeing are two different things. Their ideas may be dead wrong, and have no basis in fact. But if you cannot accept your children's ideas as theirs, they will not express themselves to you. If you can accept your children's thoughts, you can then help them to work through their ideas.

For instance, your teenager walks into the kitchen and says, "Mom, I'm thinking about moving into an apartment with three of my friends." You ask, "What friends?" He says "Bill, Susie, and Mary." You respond, "You've got to be kidding! That's the dumbest idea I've heard in a long time." By immediately denying the idea, and responding from your own emotions you cut off conversation and communication with your teenager.

This doesn't mean you should say, "Oh, good! Now I don't have to do your laundry." It *does* mean that you respond without attacking your teenager's ability to think and without implying he is an immoral slob before finding out what indeed is the case.

An answer that could lead toward more communication, eventual understanding, and maybe even different behavior, might be, "That's interesting. Tell me why you're thinking about making such a move." Further questions might lead into a good discussion of your values and his, of his ability to make decisions, his level of responsibility, the implications for his continued involvement in his church, and the impact on his friends, including the ones he is thinking about moving in with. The important thing is to let your children know that you accept their ideas and that you will encourage them to think about what they are saying.

Encourage and Affirm Your Children

Encourage your children to talk, not only about sex, but about all of the things that interest them. You affirm them when you listen carefully as your children talk, and then try in your own words to repeat back to them what they have said. This gives them the feeling that they have really been heard and can talk more. This kind of active listening remedies the most common teenage complaint about their parents—one that is often heard from younger children as well—"They don't understand me." As you listen to them, your children know that you love them and try to understand them.

If you affirm your children as persons, letting them know that you respect them, they will tend to live up to your respect. If they feel that you value their ideas, their ideas will become more valuable. They will want to share ideas that they are proud of and you will have a bigger window into what they are thinking and how they are changing. Stimulate your children to ponder issues, rather than to parrot what you or others say.

Praise is one form of affirmation, so applaud your children freely, whenever possible. If they give a thoughtful answer to a question you ask, you might say, "That's a good point. I'm glad you're thinking about it." You are attempting to build their confidence in responding to difficult subjects.

Ask Open Questions of Your Children
Questions that can be answered with a simple Yes or No tend to kill conversation. For instance, if you ask a question like, "Does the Bible agree with your idea?" you are likely to imply to your child that he is wrong. You can restate the question to encourage your child to discover what the Bible has to say. "What have you found in Scripture that has a bearing on your idea?" Other open questions are "What people are likely to be affected by the decision you are making?" "What consequences could you predict if you carry out your contemplated changes?" "How do you think other people involved might respond?" and most importantly, "Why do you feel that this idea is important?" "How much do you value this relationship or that idea?"

Avoid Conversational Barriers
If you sincerely desire free conversation with your children, you will want to avoid words and actions that cut communication. I

want to suggest five communication barriers.

1. "Gunpowder words." Gunpowder words are words that immediately incite an explosive reaction in a child or teenager. They tend to make a child angry rather than responsive. For instance, "Only boys with perverted minds ask questions like that," or "I suppose you learned that from your *nice* friends at school." Using sentences loaded with gunpowder will put your child on the defensive instead of encouraging communication. The two of you will end up waging a war of words instead of helping each other grow.

Other gunpowder words are *always, never,* and *all.* They exaggerate and rarely represent the truth. They also tend to attack a person's character. "All non-Christians are like that." Words such as these set you at odds with your children. They can easily think of exceptions to the generalizations you have made. When you generalize, it is more difficult for you to communicate accurately. You may also lessen your child's trust in you.

2. Silence. Silence is like a mask that wears a smile if worn one way but a frown if turned upside down. Silence can serve you well or it can be a dangerous weapon. Types of silence to avoid are withheld words, undertalk, superficial talk, or the silent treatment.

These are some examples of unhealthy silences in the answers to children's questions. *"Where do babies come from?" "God brings them."* Although it is true that God designed conception and childbirth, a short answer like "God brings them" is a put-off. You are saying, "I really don't want to answer your question." *"Why is homosexuality wrong?" "Because it is."* or *"The Bible says so."* This kind of answer says, "Don't ask me questions I don't think I can answer right now." A more honest answer might be, "I don't know. Let's see if we can find out in our Bibles." *"What were you and Daddy doing in there?" "It's none of your business."* Maybe it is none of a child's business what you were doing in another room, but withholding correct information or tiptoeing around an issue makes your child feel rejected or wonder if he is not good enough to be trusted with complete answers. Sidestepping a subject rather than discussing it teaches your child to give you vague answers to your questions.

Do you have trouble getting your child to talk to you? Maybe you wonder what is going through your youngster's mind about sex. In many families, one or more members are quiet and withdrawn. What do you do in that case? Pressuring a child into talking usually pushes him away even more. Being available to your child when he or she does talk, asking open questions, accepting feelings and ideas, making sure you listen carefully without condemning—these are ways to encourage a withdrawn child or teenager to feel comfortable.

While one teenage girl was opening up to her mother about her friends, she even dared to tell her mom about a certain guy who had been shockingly forward. That hit the shock button and her mother responded in anger, "I told you not to hang around with that crowd anyway!" This teenager didn't disclose any more of her dating struggles to her mother for a long time.

3. Overtalk. If a parent gives out too much information in too short a time he may overwhelm a child. If a parent harps on a subject too much, especially in the area of morality, he may irritate rather than give food for thought. Nagging will probably incite a rebellious attitude. It is better to state ideas clearly, give good support for them, and try to not force a child to think just like his parents. The parents' model of exemplary behavior and values is more convincing than talk, talk, talk. "Don't talk so much. You keep putting your foot in your mouth. Be sensible and turn off the flow" (Prov. 10:19, LB).

4. Quarreling. When you discuss sexuality with your children, they will not always agree with you. Especially so if you have not discussed the topic until they are in their teenage years. Your daughter may feel it's perfectly fine to kiss a boy on their first date. If you disagree, discuss it calmly. Differences of opinion are inevitable. And when a parent allows his anger to intrude into the conversation and attacks his teenager's character or personality, the communication flow immediately shuts off. This is quarreling. Rather than emotionally telling your daughter that she is wrong, you might ask her why she feels as she does and then share your feelings with her in a quiet manner.

5. *Poor eye contact*. Nonverbal communication is a great percentage of the total communication that goes on between two people. One important aspect of nonverbal communication is eye contact. You seem more trustworthy to your children if you look them straight in the eye. This will let them know that you value their attention, that you expect their trust, and that you are trustworthy. This means that sometimes you have to stop working so that you can turn and face your child as you talk with him, giving your full attention. Face-to-face conversations with your child, not just side-by-side conversations, are very important.

In summary, be yourself as much as you can in conversations about sexuality. Express your own ideas and feelings and encourage your child to express his. Ask questions, especially open ones. Praise, encourage, and affirm your child. Avoid the kind of communication that tends to shut off your children's ideas and feelings. Allow yourself the luxury and enjoyment of involvement in your children's lives through talking with them, rather than at them. You will be glad you did!

6

A Happy Beginning

How do you respond to your child's question, "Where do babies come from?" Two five-year-olds at church were obviously annoyed by the new babies added to the Nursery Department. They were overheard talking.

Johnny: Where do all those babies come from?

Jimmy: I dunno. I asked my Dad that question.

Johnny: What did he say?

Jimmy: He doesn't know. He told me to go ask my Mom.

Johnny: What did she say?

Jimmy: She told me some crazy story about an egg and a sperm.

When is a good time to begin talking with your children about sexuality? Some parents wait until just before marriage, when they try to give their daughter or son a one-or two-hour sex education lecture. Parents who wait that long will probably find that their children already know most of what they were going to tell them. They may, however, have to spend some time destroying preconceptions and misconceptions.

Many parents wait to talk about sexuality until their children are teenagers and begin dating. But by this time most teenagers have experienced menstruation, wet dreams, or other signs of puberty and have gathered enough misinformation to develop tremendous fears or wrong attitudes toward sex. Some who have learned about birth control are already experimenting sexually. So how early do you start sex education?

Sex education is a process that needs to start before a baby is born, as father and mother talk with each other and make preparations for the kind of atmosphere and attitude in which they plan to raise their family, especially regarding sexual matters. Then they will have a plan for the nurture and giving of love and attention a baby needs.

Some of the issues a couple may want to discuss even before the baby's birth are: (1) their own attitudes about sexuality; (2) their ability to talk about sex; (3) their feelings about handling, cuddling, and diaper-changing babies; (4) impending schedule changes; (5) expressing their love to their baby; and (6) the atmosphere of their own relationship and how it will affect their baby.

An early start on sex education is important because the child is not the only one who will get an education. Parenting is learned too—and the teachers are children. The trust and closeness that encourage children to ask their parents questions about birth, sex, and life do not just happen. They are the result of the investment parents make right from the beginning in feeding, cuddling, and playing with their baby. As parents invest, babies reward them with smiles, coos, and attention—and parents learn to love their babies. This bonding is essential for later openness in communication.

Parents, especially fathers in our culture, need to invest as much time as possible in this early bonding, not only because it is directly tied to later sex education, but because it is foundational to all parent-child relationships.

Twos and Threes
The second and third years of life are especially crucial for a child in developing relationships with people. During these years a baby begins to experience self-control and being controlled. Up until this time the baby responded pretty much to the needs that he felt from inside such as hunger or thirst, cold and other discomforts. But in their twos and threes, children begin to sense that parents often act

in reaction to them. As they sense this they begin to experience losses and gains in power. The fact that everybody needs love is well documented. But another need that everyone has (even little babies) is that of power.

Ralph Echkett, a well-known family relations counselor, puts it this way: "Because of their own helplessness, children need to have power over something in order to develop a sense of adequacy and overcome their feelings of inferiority to the older children and adults who surround them. They attempt to exercise power over their parents and it is undoubtedly good to give in to some of these demands. Parents spoil their children only when they give in to unreasonable demands as well as reasonable ones lest they lose their children's love. A firm No with affection helps children learn that it is better to have power *with people* and power over things" (*Sex Attitudes in the Home,* National Board of YMCA). Having power and learning what to do with it are lifelong tasks that start at an early age.

For the past 20 years, in response to growing permissiveness, evangelical leaders have been stressing the need that children and parents have for discipline. Some have gone as far as to say that parents are responsible to "break a child's will." While lack of discipline can lead to later selfishness and inability to tell right from wrong, breaking a child's will implies bringing a child to the point where he does not have the ability to say No or the ability to make a decision. On one extreme are parents who are unable to say No to their children, and at the other extreme are children who are unable to say No to anybody.

In terms of sex education, the results of parents being unable to say No to their children are teenagers who expect their every desire to be fulfilled. They cannot understand a date who says No to them, and so they try to overpower or manipulate that person to give in. They tend to understand love and sex in terms of "getting" or "having," not in terms of "giving."

Children who are unable to say No, and who do not learn decision-making, grow into teenagers who find it impossible to say No to dates who are interested in conquering them sexually. If they have not been allowed to have some measure of power in interpersonal relationships as children, they have not learned to control power. They tend to feel impotent and powerless.

As these children become teenagers they are likely to respond in either of two ways. (1) They become overdependent seeing themselves as worthless, powerless, and unable to control. They demand love but find giving love difficult if not impossible. They are distrustful and defensive. (2) They rebel and act out their anger over their powerlessness. They alienate their friends, and they may use sexuality to hurt those they feel have kept them powerless.

It is vitally important that two- and three-year-olds begin to learn respect for others and self-respect. The way they cope with frustration, victory, obedience, and responsibility will carry into later childhood and teenage relationships. A parent can facilitate this learning by having enough respect for his child and being strong enough as a person to allow his child to periodically say No. Then if the child faces the natural consequences of his own decision, he is likely to find his parents have some good reasons for their decisions.

Conversations with young children take special thought. Little children like to ask *Why* questions. They can drive their parents batty asking *Why* when their questions have already been answered. They often keep this up for a long time, ignoring the answers that Daddy tries so hard to accurately give.

But that does not mean that parents should quit answering the *Why* questions. If you inhibit the asking of *Why,* your children will lose some of their curiosity about life and begin to think in ruts.

After answering two or three *Whys* as best I can, I ask my children, "What do *you* think?" or "Why do *you* think a person would do that?" If they are still seriously interested in an answer, they will suggest a reason. If they are just playing a game, they will come back with an irrelevant remark and you can both have a good laugh.

Anatomical Differences
First conversations about sexuality are usually in response to questions about anatomical differences. Small children begin to notice

the parent of the opposite sex or other children who are built differently from themselves. They have already become conscious of differences in height, weight, and voice. Two-year-olds often equate height with maturity; to them the tallest person is the oldest.

As a little boy sees his father naked, he realizes that Dad is bigger than he is, but that they both have the same anatomy. When he sees Mommy, he comes to the realization that he is different from Mommy and maybe from little or big sister too. Little girls seeing their daddy realize that they have some body parts that are different from his and that they are missing some of the things that he has. This is frequently a concern and a matter of curiosity for children.

When Matthew was two, my wife asked him to pick up his toys while she was in the den changing the baby's diapers. Instead of going to his room immediately, he came up to her and asked her, "Where's Molly's penis?" She knew he hadn't yet picked up in his room and answered him, "Go pick up your toys." As he was walking out of the room, she heard him mutter to himself, "Oh, I guess she's broken."

As the function of bowel training becomes less conscious, the attention of the child focuses more and more on the genital organs. Children realize that pleasant sensations come from this area of the body. Masturbation is fairly common at this stage of development.

The genital difference between boys and girls is a matter of wonder and concern to children. Frequently they work out explanations for themselves through imaginings and dreams. One of the most common fantasies is that a boy and girl both start life with a penis, but the girl loses hers as a punishment for enjoying sensations coming from the sex organ (Helen I. Driver, Ed. *Sex Guidance for Your Child,* Madison, Wisconsin: Monora Publications, 1960, pp. 61-62).

At this early time in sex education, parents can try to respond consistently by taking the attitude that curiosity about one's body is natural. Curiosity about reproductive organs is part of that basic curiosity.

Some very positive and true answers to questions about

anatomical differences could be: "God made us this way. We're different from each other. That's the way that He designed us. Isn't God great? Isn't God good?" Or, "God in His perfect wisdom made us so that we can be happy and enjoy life with other people. God made faces. God made hands and fingers. God made feet and toes. God made arms and legs and bodies and God made penises and vaginas. We can thank God for the way that He made us. Let's thank God together right now for making you just the way He made you, OK?"

When you respond positively to questions about anatomical differences and sexual curiosity, you can avoid the kind of repression children get into when parents avoid answering their questions or tell them not to talk about "those kinds of things." When you respond openly and honestly to your children, they feel free about asking more questions, now and as they grow older.

Waiting for a New Baby

The coming of a baby brother or sister is an excellent opportunity for sex education for two- and three-year-olds. Even little ones will notice that Mommy is getting bigger around the tummy and will ask questions. The children can be prepared for this tremendous occasion well before Mommy shows her pregnancy.

Not many two- or three-year-olds are interested in the details of conception But one aspect of pregnancy is a source of tremendous curiosity and amazement for two- and three-year-olds—the relative size of a fetus. Seeing pictures of an embryo appropriate for the time of pregnancy, and watching that unborn baby become larger as the time progresses, helps a two- or three-year-old understand and share in the expectancy of a baby brother or sister.

If a baby is going to be your last child, you will not have the coming of a baby brother or sister to help you with his sex education. However, you may be able to accomplish much of the same in terms of explanations and opportunities for dialogue by taking advantage of the birth of one of your friend's babies. It is not as intimate and your friends may have reservations about letting your son or daughter feel the unborn baby kick, but some of the same openness can be accomplished.

Teach by Positive Concepts

Related to the discovery of anatomical differences is the tendency of young children to show off their genitals. Parents who discover this activity easily overreact, reading in more than what is happening. It is very easy to be negative in this circumstance, telling children that what they are doing is wrong. It is more difficult to calmly give them some reasons why this activity is wrong and offer them positive alternatives.

Little children's concepts of right and wrong are gained directly from their parents. What is right is what Mother and Father approve. What is wrong is what they obviously disapprove. So when a mother or father brand something as wrong, they need to tell their children why it is wrong and what is the proper behavior. Here parents should be very careful that children do not generalize, from disapproving behavior, that anything having to do with sexuality is bad.

That God made human bodies very special is a positive concept. The idea of respecting one's own body and other people's bodies enough to wear clothes and not to show off to others is a positive concept. The idea that there are some very special things that are talked about only in the family is a positive concept. These simple ideas will help keep sex education within the family instead of all over the neighborhood.

Some parents ask if a child should be spanked for showing off his genitals. "Shouldn't we help them realize the gravity of their behavior?" they ask. "If we don't spank, they might to it again." Ask yourself, *Just how grave is it?* For a two- or three-year-old to be proud of his whole body is natural. If he understands that another child is different from him he may want to explore some of the differences. Will this behavior change? Yes, as they get a little older, children naturally become secretive and discreet about their bodies.

Our four-year-old happened to be changing clothes one evening recently when some of our friends popped in for a few minutes. We went to the door to welcome them in and then she heard us all coming toward her room to show them her new wallpaper. So she dove under the bed and stayed there without making a sound the whole time we were in her room. After a while we missed her and began looking around. We found her still under her bed in her slip.

Fours and Fives

A recent conversation on sexuality with our five-year-old daughter, Molly, was so illuminating that I initiated another one, this time with a tape recorder. Our conversation, which follows illustrates some interesting and typical aspects of sex education with preschoolers.

First, no matter how open a family is in its discusson of life, birth, and sexuality, children find these topics difficult to discuss. They are curious and want to learn, but they're uncomfortable bringing up these topics themselves. This "embarrassment" will not tend to decrease over time, unless parents take the initiative in discussing sexuality with their children. Note too that Molly was somewhat conscious of the tape recorder, especially at the beginning of the conversation. She was less inhibited in our prior untaped conversation.

Second, since we had discussed anatomical differences, pregnancy, and birth with Molly more than conception, she found these areas easier to talk about.

. Third, although some families keep discussions on sexuality between mother and daughter and between father and son, we are not afraid of "oedipal" or other conflicts some parents worry might arise as a result of father-daughter or mother-son discussions. We want our children to see the strengths of our love relationship for each other and for them. We want them to realize that we are not going to let our embarrassment stop us from discussing in our family the things that need to be discussed.

Fourth, we use drawings in our sex education. Children think in concrete terms and verbal descriptions simply leave too much area for misunderstanding.

Fifth, we keep sex within the context of love, marriage, and

God's design for human behavior.

Sixth, it is acceptable to sidetrack and talk about other things. We make time to follow our children's trains of thought—even onto sidetracks. We get back to other aspects of sexuality in future conversations. In the meantime, we can teach them about other special parts of God's creation.

Seventh, we talk directly to God in many of our conversations with each other. Prayer does not need to be reserved only for Sunday School and before meals. And now, my conversation with Molly.

Molly: Where did I come from?

Dad: Right, where did you come from? Can you tell me?

Molly: Mommy's tummy.

Dad: Mommy's tummy. You mean, she ate you?

Molly: No.

Dad: No? What happened? How did you get into Mommy's tummy?

Molly: I don't know.

Dad: You don't remember?

Molly: No.

Dad: Remember we talked about how it takes a mommy and a daddy.

Molly: Oh yes, that's how.

Dad: Then what?

Molly: No way, I'm not going to tell you that. No way!

Dad: Why not?

Molly: It's embarrassing.

Dad: It's embarrassing? It's something very special. Something that we don't talk about outside our family. But *we* can talk about it—you and I.

Molly: But I don't want to talk about it 'cause Mommy's in there.

Dad: Oh, because Mommy's in there. Well, she can't hear us. We'll just talk about it—you and me.

Molly: (giggles)

Dad: OK, tell me what you remember.

Molly: I remember this. (Drawing of a man and a woman in bed under the covers.)

Dad: Oh, OK.

Molly: This is the starting of it.

Dad: This is the starting. . . . OK.

Molly: Look at this. (Drawing of man and woman in bed, facing each other, man over woman)

Dad: Well, what's happening here?

Molly: I don't want to tell you. I don't want to tell you. No way.

Dad: Why not?

Molly: 'Cause.

Dad: Do you want me to tell you?

Molly: Uh Huh. (affirmative)

Dad: OK. A mommy and a daddy sleep together 'cause they love each other very much.

Molly: Yeah, but I didn't know all that you had to do was love each other. . . . (giggles)

Dad: Well that's the first and most important thing. Sometimes men and women don't love each other and they have babies and you know what happens?

Molly: What?

Dad: They might not love their babies either.

Molly: I love my baby.

Dad: Hmmm. . . what's your baby's name?

Molly: I got, I got. . . My baby?

Dad: Hmm Hum. (affirmative)

Molly: I got, probably about 12 babies.

Dad: Twelve babies! You have some very nice dolls.

Molly: More than 12 babies. I got one dog too.

Dad: Yes, a dog and a monkey and . . .

Molly: Georgiana?

Dad: Is she a monkey?

Molly: She's a monkey. And this doll right here. And I used to have dogs named Cammy and Meggan, but we gave Meggan away and Cammy died.

Dad: That's right.

Molly: Not baby Meggan.

Dad: Right, when Cammy had her puppies, do you know how she had her puppies?

Molly: How?

Dad: The same way, pretty much, that mommys and daddys have little boys and girls.

Molly: I know it.

Dad: OK, so it starts with love. . . .

Molly: Yeah, but the dogs can't name them.

Dad: No, that's why we name them.

Molly: Yeah, 'cause the dogs can't talk.

Dad: Right.

Molly: They just say "wuff" but they don't say anything else.

Dad: Dogs' tongues are very long so they can lick up their food and stuff.

Molly: Yeah, like dog food.

Dad: But since their tongues are so long they can't talk with them. Aren't you glad that God made your tongue shorter so you can use it to talk with?

Molly: Hmm hum. (affirmative)

Dad: Me too. Let's thank God for our hands and our tongues, OK?

Molly: OK.

Dad: Do you want to thank God for your hands or your tongue?

Molly: Tongue.

Dad: OK, I'll thank God for our hands.

Molly: OK.

Dad: I'll go first.

Molly: No, I will.

Dad: OK, go ahead.

Molly: Dear Lord, thank You for tongues. In Jesus name. Amen.

Dad: Dear heavenly Father, thank You for our hands. Thank You for making us so wonderfully. In Jesus name. Amen.

In summary, if you start your sex education early it will be easier as your children grow to continue with less embarrassment to them or to you as parents.

7

The School Years

Anna and Bill were third-grade friends. Anna enjoyed playing at Bill's house once in a while, since they lived near each other. Bill even began to give Anna little presents, like a glass dog and a small china dish. Anna did not understand why he did that, but she never gave it much thought. Then one spring afternoon on the way home from school, Bill kissed Anna on the lips. She pulled away in horror. "How could you do that?" she shrieked. "I don't ever want to see you again!" She ran home as fast as she could and threw away every present Bill had given her. That kiss so thoroughly disgusted her that it ended a good friendship.

School children, ages 6 to 11, develop their own ways of looking at life. Their autonomy has developed to the point that they now interpret events from their own perspectives. They are fascinated with their world, exploring and discovering facts and always testing their competence. They ask a mountain of questions—unless they have learned that their parents won't answer. Then they may take questions to their teachers and—more than anyone else—to their friends.

When preteens ask questions about sex they are usually motivated by curiosity to know the facts. Their own sexuality is less of a motivating force than it was in early childhood or than it will be when they become adolescents. Psychologists sometimes call this the "latent" period of growth. Boys want to play with boys, and girls want to play with girls. Before and after these years, children experiment, feel, and discover sexuality. This age group wants to *know* about sex, to accumulate facts. As they shoot up with physical growth, they also burst with intellectual growth.

As curiosity becomes other-centered more than self-centered, individual differences are noticed and often questioned. You might hear comments like, "Oh look, they're kissing!" and "Why is she in that wheelchair?" The sight of animals mating arouses intense curiosity. A new world of laughter is opened with primitive "dirty jokes" usually starting with plays on words associated with elimination and reproduction.

As parents, we need to understand our children, and to anticipate their stages of growth and be ready to help them as they arrive. Our children depend on us to teach and guide them; but we can't do that effectively unless we know them. A major factor in sex education at this age is the teaching of respect, of awe, for the way God has made us. Then sexuality becomes a sacred aspect of all of life instead of a shameful part of sinful behavior. Sex can be seen as God-given and beautiful instead of as an unforgivable sin or dirty.

As school age children become more interested in others, their natural tendency to compare produces a higher degree of self-consciousness, and they learn to hide their true emotions. After all, to let other children see them crying or fearful is threatening. Boys are learning "machismo" and girls are learning how to "keep a stiff upper lip." They feel pressured to act more like adults. Consequently, a young boy balks at sitting on his mother's lap or pulls away when she tries to kiss him good night. This does not mean he dislikes his mother, but that he is struggling to act more grown up.

Another characteristic of this age group is the tendency to relate better with the same sex. Younger children have little concern for the gender of their playmates, but as they absorb gender identification in their homes, they generally prefer companionship with their own sex. Exceptions to this do not necessarily indicate psychological problems or homosexuality.

Each child grows in every way at his or her own rate, and rates of growth are quite irregular. Some growth comes quickly, some at a snail's pace. This is true of emotional, relational, spiritual, and intellectual growth, as well as physical growth.

The end of the latency period is the onset of puberty and entrance into the junior high scene. Puberty is thought of as sudden change, and some sudden changes do take place. But in the fourth, fifth, and sixth grades, the gradual growth that leads to puberty is causing many other changes to take place in a child's life. During these years parents can be especially helpful in preparing their children for puberty and adolescence.

If sex education has been put off and a child is in fifth or sixth grade, it is now imperative! The child will have some brand new experiences that may be frightening or shaming if he or she is not prepared for them.

You don't have to schedule a formal time for a teaching session on sexuality, unless that is the only way to bring yourself to broach the subject. You have many opportunities to teach, if you accept them casually in your everyday life. Bible study can provide some handy springboards for sex education conversations. For instance discussing the meaning of "Adam *knew* Eve and she conceived" might start a good conversation. Defining terms like *fornication, adultery, virgin birth, lust, begat,* etc., with a careful dialogue instead of a quick definition, can lead to memorable teaching-learning experiences together.

What to Teach and How

Since the facts of sexuality and birth are an important aspect of sex education during the school years, the rest of this chapter concentrates on specific facts to teach your children and ways to teach them.

1. Family. Children need to take an objective look at families, including their own, to appreciate family life. Then they may be better able to value sexuality as a part of family life. Study of biblical families together, fellowship with other families, and especially regular "family night home" traditions can develop this value.

It is important that children who are believers see themselves as part of God's forever family and experience some of His benefits. By doing this, they can actualize their faith relationship with God in ways they can understand. Studying a book like *Characteristics of a Caring Home* by Norman Wright and Rex Johnson (Santa Ana, California: Vision House Publishers, 1979) can aid this type of study.

Facts to teach: Not all boys and girls get married when they grow up, but most do. If a couple decides to have a baby, and they can have one (some couples cannot for medical reasons), they become parents when the woman conceives and a baby starts to grow in the mother's womb.

Some families include just two people, a husband and wife. Some include a father, mother, and children and are called primary families. Lots of families include grandparents, several aunts, uncles, and cousins, in addition to the parents and children. These are called extended families. In the United States and Canada there are more primary families than extended families. As the family of God, the church is much like one big extended family.

The Bible shows how family members are to interact with each other in passages such as Deuteronomy 6, Ephesians 5 and 6, Philippians 4, Colossians 3.

2. Elimination. As children grow older and learn privacy about keeping their genitals covered and using the toilet, parents need to make sure they express a healthy respect for normal functions, rather than an attitude of embarrassment. Talking about elimination in a factual way, using correct terms rather than slang, can help a child have a good attitude toward himself and others.

Facts to teach: Every living thing must get rid of its waste. Plants breathe in carbon dioxide and give off oxygen. Animals and people eat food, drink liquid, and eliminate what their bodies do not need.

Animals and humans discard their solid wastes through defecating and their liquid wastes through urinating. Both men and women defecate through the opening between their legs called the anus. A man urinates through the opening in his penis (urethra), and a woman urinates through an opening called the urethra. Her urethra is near her vagina, but is not the same opening.

Think how fat and poisoned we would be if God had not designed this marvelous system. We can thank God for making us so intricately! The Psalmist David wrote, "For Thou didst form my inward parts; Thou didst weave me in my mother's womb" (Ps. 139:13, NASB). The Hebrew word for inward parts is literally kidneys. Our kidneys are part of our elimination system.

3. The reproductive system. Even very young children are aware of some characteristics that make men and women different from each other. But many school age children do not know the functions of the various reproductive organs.

As children grow into the "pubescent" years, 8-11, they are usually ready to learn more details about the inner anatomy and functions of the reproductive system. Here a diagram is worth a thousand words.

Facts to teach: A woman has two ovaries, sometimes called female sex organs, that are walnut-sized located in her abdomen on each side of her uterus. These organs produce eggs that are released into the fallopian tubes and hormones which are secreted directly into her blood stream.

About once a month a ripe egg or ovum, about the size of the dot on this *i*, is released by the ovary and swept up the fallopian tube toward the uterus..

Most women produce about 400 of these ova during their lifetime. Of course, only a few will become babies. The rest continue along the fallopian tube to the uterus or womb. The uterus is approximately in the center of the lower abdomen, is about three inches long, and looks much like a small pear turned upside down. The uterus is where a baby grows for nine months before it is born.

An egg that is *not* going to become a baby flows out of the uterus through an opening at the bottom of the uterus called the cervix, then through the vagina, a tube that is about three and one half inches long. This tube ends at the vulva or exterior opening. The vagina also serves as the tube into which a woman's husband fits his penis when they are having intercourse or "making love." His sperm in a fluid called semen are ejaculated or spurted into his wife's vagina from where they may swim up through her uterus into her fallopian tubes. If one of the sperm unites with an egg that is being swept down the tube, that is called fertilization of the egg, and is the beginning of a new life.

The fertilized egg continues to be swept down the fallopian tube where it becomes buried in the wall of the uterus. There it will grow into a baby, getting its nourishment from the uterus wall. Eight weeks after the conception of the child, a special organ called the placenta develops. The growing baby gets its food and oxygen through this organ which also acts as a filter to screen out most chemicals that would harm the baby.

When the baby is ready for birth, the wall of the uterus begins contracting or squeezing and the baby is pushed out through the cervix and vagina, usually head first. This is painful, but if a mother has properly prepared for the birth of her child she can greatly reduce the pain and find the birth a rewarding experience. The anticipated joy of being able to see and hold her baby helps her do the work and endure the pain of giving birth.

A man's sex cells, called sperm, are very different from a woman's. Sperm are much smaller than eggs, and they have small tails which propel them. They resemble little tadpoles.

The sperm cells are made by two glands called testicles, which are located on the outside of the man's body. (See diagram.) These are held in two pouches of skin (or scrotum) which hang between his legs behind the penis. The penis is three to five inches long and is thicker than a man's thumb. The penis has two major jobs. A man urinates through his penis; and he puts his sperm into a woman's vagina through it. The two jobs never happen at the same time, and thus sperm and urine cannot mix together.

At birth, the end of a boy's penis has a layer of skin covering it. A doctor may cut off this skin in a simple operation called circumcision. This makes it easier to keep the penis clean and is done by Jewish people for religious reasons (Gen. 17:10-14).

A man's internal sex organs consist of the vas deferens, the seminal vesicles, and the urethra. After sperm are made in the testicles, they move through a tube called the vas deferens and then they mix with a fluid stored in the seminal vesicles (semen). Finally this fluid leaves the man's body through the urethra, a tube that ends at the tip of the penis. The other end of the urethra also leads to the bladder and is a passageway for urine to leave the body.

4. Sexual intercourse. By the time a child is in third or fourth-grade he knows that men and women go to bed together and that they have sexual intercourse. He probably has other names for it. But ask him why couples have intercourse, and unless he's parroting something someone told him earlier, the answers will probably have something to do with having babies and having fun.

Before they get to the teenage years, children need to understand the purposes of sex as God designed it. Letha Scanzoni suggests four purposes for sexual intercourse. They are: (1) procreation—the vehicle God designed for reproduction of species; (2) communication—expressing unity, intimacy, and vulnerability; (3) recreation. To quote John White, "The physical side of sex is only part of a larger whole . . . the first purpose of sex is the ending of isolation and loneliness. And loneliness can only end where trust exists—trust that someone has made a commitment to me and I to that person in a sworn covenant until death parts us. Within such a relationship the physical pleasures of sex may blossom and mysteriously deepen to solidify the relationship (*Eros Defiled,* Downers Grove, Illinois: InterVarsity Press, 1977, p. 11). (4) Release—the expression of sexual drives and energies.

As God designed it, sex is sacred and good. When we misuse it, sex, like anything else God designed that we corrupt and misuse, becomes sinful. Four ways sex is commonly misused are: (1) to punish—to get even with parts of self that are not acceptable. Rapists are usually using sex to punish; (2) to control—to keep one's partner in a dependent situation; (3) to profit—prostitutes and pimps use sex to make money; (4) to gratify—taking recreation and release beyond God's design to the point that people are used as objects to gratify one's impulses.

Facts to teach: Sexual intercourse was designed by God for a husband and wife to express their love to each other creatively and enjoy the pleasure each can receive from the other. It is not only to have babies, but may be enjoyed throughout married life.

When sexual intercourse is misused, the result is pollution of people's spirits by neglect or cruelty, of their bodies by disease, and of their relationships by mistrust of their selves and by alienation or loneliness.

Sexual intercourse was designed by God to happen when a husband and wife excite each other's emotions by being very close to each other physically by hugging, holding, touching, and kissing each other. As they do this, the man's penis becomes stiff and erect as more blood than usual rushes into its tissues. Also lubricating fluids are secreted into the woman's vagina.

When they are both ready, the man and woman put their penis and vagina together, and the man gently slides his penis into the woman's vagina. All of this feels very good to both of them if they are being gentle, respectful, and loving, and if they are aroused by each other.

As the man and woman move their hips back and forth, and their penis and vagina rub against each other, they get more and more excited until either or both of them come to what is called a climax. For the man, climax means that a thick, sticky fluid called semen flows into the woman's vagina. This fluid carries his sperm. For the woman, climax means that the muscles in her abdomen contract repeatedly and involuntarily. God made sexual intercourse to be one of the most pleasureable things a man or a woman can ever experience. Where other things that are fun can get old and boring, sexual intercourse, for a husband and wife who love each other, can be thrilling all of their lives together!

After climax comes a time of restful relaxation during which a couple who love each other feel very close, cuddly, even dreamy. It is a time of appreciation and thankfulness—to each other and to God.

5. *Growth and puberty*. Children are involved daily in the process of growing, yet it helps them to know the overall picture of growth. Let them know that the growth rate varies in each child, and that for Susie's breasts to develop much later than Karen's is

very normal.

Facts to teach: All living things grow and mature. Puberty is a special time of growth when the body produces hormones which cause boys and girls to undergo a number of physical changes. Boys will see that their sex organs grow in size; their voices deepen; hair will grow on their faces, around their genitals, and other places on their bodies; they may have problems with acne as their skin becomes oilier. The testicles at this time start to make sperm. A boy's penis sometimes will fill with blood and enlarge, causing an erection. Both boys and girls at this time have an increased interest in the opposite sex.

At puberty girls will notice that their breasts become larger; they will eventually begin to menstruate; hair will grow on their bodies, especially around their genitals and their voice pitch may change. Girls as well may have acne problems.

6. Menstruation. Sally was a 12-year-old junior high school student. Her teacher and her parents had carefully explained menstruation to her. When she started to bleed for the first time during a gym class, she quietly excused herself and did what her mother had advised her to do. She returned to the class feeling a little frightened but happy with herself. She knew that a good thing had just happened to her.

This is the kind of preparation that parents can give their children. Too often the opposite occurs, when a girl does not know how to react to her first "period." Most schools teach children about this topic and have good resource materials, such as films and books. Yet because the subject is so delicate, parents definitely should discuss menstruation with their own children, and make certain that both sons and daughters have their questions answered.

When a girl begins to menstruate, it is such a major change that it can affect her emotions significantly. One good way to open up the topic for discussion would be for the mother to show her daughter a sanitary napkin or tampon. Then she could start from the child's natural curiosity to know what is in the package. "Have you seen these before? Mommy uses them very often; would you like to know why?" If a child sees her mother hiding these supplies, she will probably think something is wrong and she shouldn't ask questions, or that their use is shameful.

Facts to teach: Once every month a girl will discharge a bloody fluid from her uterus. This usually begins around the ages of 10-13. The time of bleeding is called a period and usually lasts from three to seven days every 28 days (approximately). It is a normal sign of maturing. Menstruation can affect a girl's emotions temporarily, possibly making her feel a little low.

In order for menstruation to occur, an egg is released from the ovaries and, if it is not fertilized through intercourse, the rich lining of the uterus (which has built up to nourish a baby if conceived) falls away from the uterine walls, and that is the bloody fluid passed from the girl's body.

7. Ejaculation. The guilt and shame that some boys have to deal with over wet dreams or nocturnal emission can be avoided with concerned sex education during the later school years. Dad may have described ejaculation as a part of intercourse but he needs to add that as his son grows into adolescence he will probably have dreams concerning sex that will result in ejaculation. This is nothing to be ashamed of. It is quite normal, and does not mean he has wet the bed (it is not urine) or that his thoughts are necessarily lustful.

Facts to teach: As boys mature their gonads or testicles begin to produce sperm and their bodies semen. They will not know when this is happening, and cannot make it happen any sooner than it will happen. When they have more sperm and semen than their bodies need, they will have a "wet dream"—a dream that will result in "ejaculation" or spurting out of some of their semen with sperm.

They need not worry—it washes out of pajamas and sheets, and their gonads will produce more. They will not run out of sperm or semen until late in life, if ever.

Values to Sell

You have read quite a bit about what facts your children need to know. Remember, however, to dialogue rather than lecture. You don't have to teach all the facts at once. You may cover the same material several times, since there are so many concepts, emotions, and values to deal with. I also want to reemphasize the importance of using natural daily situations to teach about sex, rather than manufacturing or forcing a learning situation. Respond to your children's curiosity if they ask you questions; but if they don't, you initiate the conversations.

Behind all these amazing facts of how God planned our bodies, lies something far more crucial than the facts themselves—the values you esteem. Your children will absorb your values like sponges, and these values will be guidelines to them for a lifetime. When they redefine their values as teenagers, they will have yours as a reference point. It is essential that your values be biblical, healthy, godly ones, and that you yourself know what your values are and can articulate them. Make sure your children know that you believe that sex is a beautiful, God-created form of communication between a husband and wife who love each other. Facts can be pulled from books, but your values as parents are a precious gift to your children.

The Book of Proverbs teaches a lot about values. Concerning parents, it says: "Hear, my son, your father's instructions, and do not forsake your mother's teaching; indeed they are a graceful wreath to your head, and ornaments about your neck" (Prov. 1:8-9, NASB).

Are your values and instructions the kind that will be graceful and beautiful to your children? With God's wisdom, you can bring this kind of wealth to your sons and daughters.

Questions Your Children May Ask

Since your children will probably ask you some of the following questions, it would be well for you to think about how you want to answer them.

1. Do little boys have sperm cells? Boys do not produce sperm cells until they reach puberty because their gonads are not mature enough. Puberty generally begins some time between ages 10 and 13.

2. Does a mother get pregnant by kissing? The answer is obvious to adults, but this is a common misconception for youngsters, especially younger ones.

3. Does a mother get pregnant every time she has intercourse? No, parents usually have intercourse without pregnancy taking place. A mother's egg is only released once a month, and an egg could meet up with a sperm cell only a few days each month. When couples are not intending to have a baby, they usually use some form of birth control.

4. Why do you shut the door when you have intercourse? Intercourse is the most personal way a couple can show how much they care for each other. They want to be totally alone and undisturbed so that they can enjoy the time the most. They do not want to be watched, since intercourse is not an experience to be shared with others.

5. Why don't men menstruate? God has prepared women's · bodies to bear children. Therefore, until a baby is conceived, they need to rid their bodies of the rich lining of blood that forms each month in the uterus. Men do not become pregnant and give birth to babies. Therefore they do not menstruate.

6. Do women menstruate all their lives? Women menstruate from puberty until they are 45 or 50 years old. At that time their bodies stop releasing an egg each month. God created women so that they would not have to care for small babies in their later years when it would be difficult for them. The only other time a woman does not menstruate is during pregnancy.

7. Does menstruation hurt? Some girls have discomfort or pain and some do not. They might experience a headache or backache or abdominal cramps in the first few days of flow. They may also feel a little low emotionally. If they experience these things, they should rest for a while.

8. Can a girl play actively during menstruation? Yes, certainly. She will learn how to wear sanitary pads or tampons to keep her clothes clean, and she should bathe every day to smell fresh. Then she can do whatever she feels comfortable doing.

9. Is the bloody fluid at menstruation dirty? No. The discharge is something a girl wants to keep private, but it could not hurt anyone in any way and is not unclean.

10. What is a virgin? A virgin is a woman or girl who has never had sexual intercourse with a man. The word is also used for a boy or man who has never had sexual intercourse.

Glossary for Chapter Seven

uterus
ovaries
fallopian tubes
cervix
vagina
penis
testicles
scrotum
vas deferens
seminal vesicles
urethra
bladder
wet dreams
nocturnal emission
puberty

menstruation
period
adolescence
latent period
gonads
birth control
placenta
embryo
fertilization
sperm, semen
ovum, ova
genitals
ejaculation

intercourse
circumcision
procreation
intimacy
vulnerability
communication
elimination
reproduction
conception
fornication
adultery
virgin birth
lust
beget, begat

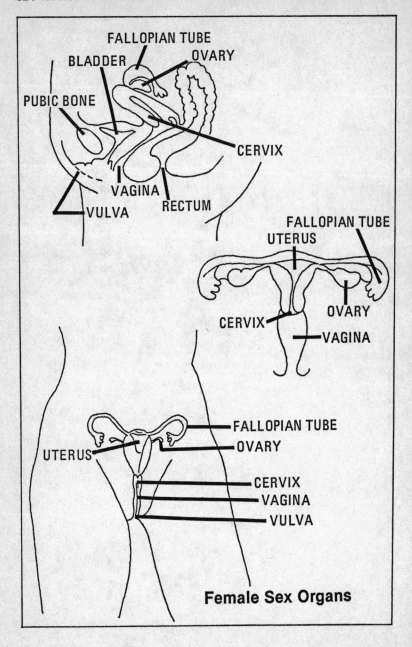

Female Sex Organs

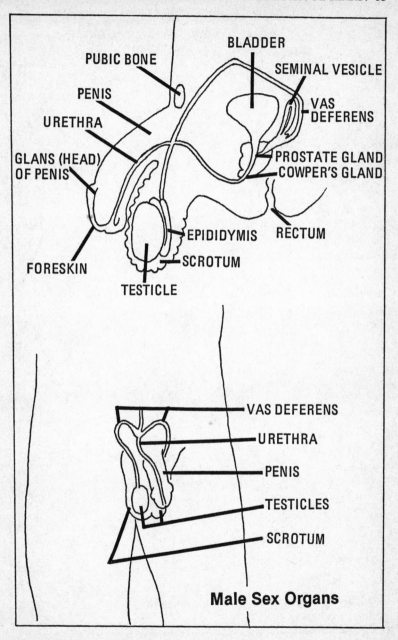

Male Sex Organs

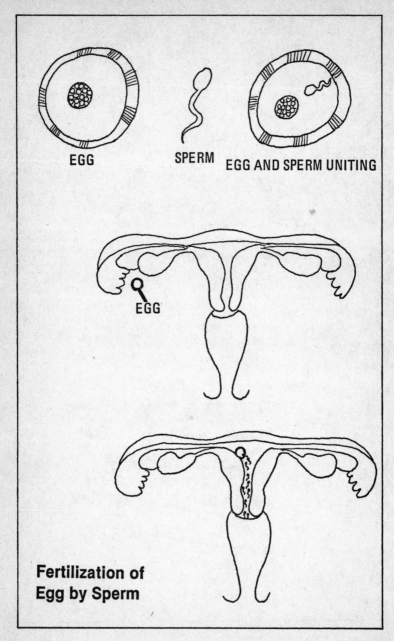

EGG   SPERM   EGG AND SPERM UNITING

EGG

Fertilization of Egg by Sperm

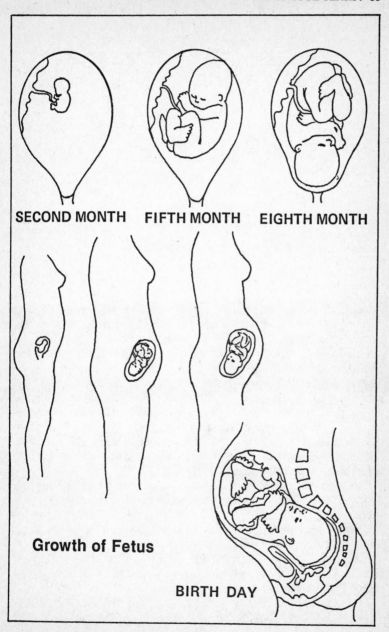

SECOND MONTH FIFTH MONTH EIGHTH MONTH

Growth of Fetus

BIRTH DAY

8

Early Adolescence

A counselor friend of mine stopped into my office one morning and asked, "What do you say to parents who come for help because their teenage daughter is so depressed over an abortion she got a couple of months ago that they are afraid that she is going to commit suicide?"

At a conference where I was speaking to college students on preparing for marriage, I distributed blank cards to the students, asking them to write down the questions they had for me. The questions ranged from one extreme to the other. Two of them were: "Do you think it is all right to kiss a boy before engagement?" and "Should I tell my fiance about my father's incest with me? Or is it something he doesn't need to know about?"

One high school girl's question at a rap session was: "All but two of my friends at school have been pregnant and had abortions. Is there something wrong with me?"

These questions illustrate the amazing spectrum of educational levels that exist by the time children become teenagers. Evangelical church groups are likely to include teenagers who have had sexual relationships and others who have very little understanding of sexuality and are fearful of the whole subject.

The Institute for Family Research and Education reported one million adolescent pregnancies in 1976 and three million new cases of venereal disease in the same year, two thirds of which were among young people under 25. (*Community Family Life Education Programs for Parents* (Syracuse: Institute for Family Research and Education, 1977, p. 46).

Senator Edward Kennedy expressed his concern over this situation in a speech to the Senate in 1975. He said, "During the past decade we have become increasingly aware of the large number of young girls who are bearing and rearing children while still at school age. Indeed, some of these young people are still children themselves. The teenage population is the only group in our society in which the number of births shows a continuing increase. . . . The number of births to girls under the age of fifteen has doubled between 1960 and 1973. In 1970 there were over 644,000 live births to girls 19 years of age and under. Of these almost one-quarter million were born to girls between the ages 15 and 17." (*Congressional Record,* October 21, 1975)

Obviously, the need for sex education continues right into the adolescent years. Whether it be a teenager who is ignorant sexually or one who has had the advantage of good sex education at home, church, and school, the important thing is not to stop.

Several questions come up during the teenage years. One concern is the physiological aspects of sexuality. Where curiosity previously motivated questions, now they are often motivated by the need to deal with problems. If you can keep your sex education at least one jump ahead of the most common problem your teenagers will face, you may be able to prevent mistakes, problems, and even heartaches. The issues and questions raised in this chapter continue to be current on into the middle teens. The focus is still preventive.

Premarital Sex

Probably the biggest issue that faces parents of teenagers is premarital sex. The Institute for Family Research and Education reports "Whatever their personal views, all parents must realize that fully half of all young people will have had sexual intercourse before they finish high school, whether we like it or not and whether they like it or not. The peer pressure for sexual involvement is enormous. The messages teenagers receive from newspapers, magazines, and especially television are extremely powerful. Parents who do not want their children to have sexual relations—a decisive majority—should let their children know how they feel. They need not be ashamed of their traditional values. Old-fashioned parents are every bit as good as newfangled ones. But all parents, regardless of orientation, must strive to obtain an unobstructed communication link with their children. To break off communications is to let children know that they cannot talk to their parents about any aspects of sexuality" (op cit., p. 19).

That fifty-fifty statistic may sound discouraging but to me it sounds encouraging. The chance that your teenager will make it to marriage without premarital sex is fifty-fifty. Those are still pretty good odds, and I think they can be improved. If you have been teaching your children responsibility throughout their lives, and building an atmosphere of openness, acceptance, love and mutual trust and encouragement, I believe the odds in your favor will increase tremendously. There is one major factor that will make a great difference. If your teenagers realize the tremendous value you place in your relationship with God through Jesus Christ; if they feel the importance you place in Scripture and what it says about morality, ethics and especially sexuality, I think that they will have a much greater chance of reaching marriage as virgins.

If you have been an open, responsive parent, one question your teenager may ask is, "Why should I wait for sex until marriage?" This question is sometimes disturbing to parents because they immediately suspect that their teenager has not waited and is wrestling with some of the implications of having not waited. The possibility that your child is wrestling with the idea of sex before submitting to the impulse is more likely. That your teenager asks you, his parents, is a compliment. Some, afraid to talk to their parents, go to a pastor or youth leader; many teenagers try to learn from each other. When teenagers ask this question of each other, the answer they often get is, "If it feels good, do it!"

How would you respond to the question, "Why wait until marriage?'' I hope you will not respond defensively or suspiciously, but will set aside time to discuss the issue in an unhurried dialogue. Some of the following perspectives might be helpful to include in such a dialogue.

1. The Bible calls premarital sex *fornication* and *sin*. If a person is sensitive to the teaching of Scripture, he will avoid premarital sex. But be careful in discussing this not to use the Bible as a weapon. The vitality of your teenager's relationship with Christ will be the decisive issue. If his relationship is weak or nonexistent, he can easily dismiss the Bible's teaching as traditional, outmoded, and irrelevant. If, however, his relationship with Christ is strong and growing, that relationship will make the Bible's teaching specific to his behavior. If you're convinced that your teenager has a growing relationship with Christ, rather than trying to convince him of the need to wait for marriage, help him find ways of making that wait easier.

2. Contrary to popular opinion, premarital sex is not an expression of love for another person. It is an expression of self-love. A teenager is really saying "I love myself and I want you to help me love me. It feels so good that I can't resist." So the question you might ask your teenager is, "Why do you love this person? Why have you chosen this person rather than others to be intimate with?" Then listen carefully for your teenager's answers. The answers are likely to suggest that this person compliments, encourages, and pays attention to your teenager. If you son responds with statements like "she dresses well," "she is pretty," "I like her personality," "she makes me feel good when I'm with her," he is really saying, "She helps me love myself."

Often these are the same reasons teenagers and young adults give for marriage. When this is the case, you can predict that as soon as they get tired of meeting each other's demands for "love," the couple is going to be ready to give up on their commitment.

A study of 1 Corinthians 13 with your teenager will help him understand that premarital sex is not an expression of love, but of selfishness. Only within the commitment of marriage does sex become the giving, growing, intimate love that God intended it to be. Questions you might ask are, "Is premarital sex patient and kind? Or, is it jealous? Does it seek its own way? Act unbecomingly?" Love bears all things, believes all things, hopes all things, endures all things (verse 7). Love never fails (verse 8). Waiting for marriage takes the kind of commitment that is described in 1 Corinthians 13:7-8.

3. The possibility of pregnancy is still a very important reason for waiting until after marriage for sexual intercourse. The most recent findings in adolescent study indicate that even though contraceptives are widely available, many adolescents do not use them because they feel this is too calculating. They are, in the face of their own mores and values, planning to be sexually active. But they would rather be surprised and overwhelmed by it.

Pregnancy then, forces choices that few adolescents and their families are ready to cope with. For instance, according to Braen and Forbush, pregnancy is still the principle reason that girls drop out of school (B. Braen & J. Forbush "School-age Parenthood—A National Overview," *The Journal of School Health,* 1975, p. 45). In terms of medical risk, mortality rates, toxemia, and premature births are higher among adolescent pregnancies. Also, their surviving infants have a 400 percent higher probability of neurological defects and retardation (J. Bemis, E. Diers, and R. Sharpe "The Teen-age Single Mother" *Child Welfare,* 1976, p. 55). Obviously the safest way to avoid premarital pregnancy is to avoid premarital sex.

4. Characteristic of many adolescents is the absence of what some writers call futurity. (John A. Bruce "Adolescent Parents: A Special Case of the Unplanned Family" *Family Coordinator,* 1978, Vol. 1, p. 75) Futurity is the ability to judge present behaviors in terms of future consequences. It's an aspect of responsibility. The ability to set priorities, to delay gratification, to make long-term investments of self are aspects of futurity. The "we can't wait, we need each other now" idea certainly lacks futurity.

5. Premarital sex clashes with the idea that marriage is a picture of God's relationship with His people. A relationship with God through Jesus Christ starts with His commitment to us and our

commitment to follow Him. This is pictured by the wedding ceremony where a couple publicly commit themselves to each other in marriage. Premarital sex has no counterpart in a person's relationship with God because God certainly is a stranger to all who have not established, by commitment, a personal relationship with Him.

You can probably think of other perspectives that are particularly relevant to your own family and relationships. You need to be careful not to overwhelm a teenager with all of these reasons, thereby coming across as a school teacher or lecturer. A dialogue or a series of dialogues will give your teenagers the impression that you respect their ability to think with you, that you respect them as persons, and that you invest in them instead of just laying down laws for them. You are not likely to convince your teenagers with your logic. You may win them with your love and understanding.

How Far Can I Go?

When a teenager has commited himself or herself not to "go all the way" the next question is "How far can I go?" Before considering responses to this question, ask yourself "How far did I go, sexually, before marriage?" If your teens could have seen your earlier dating behavior, would they accept the standards you are suggesting to them now? Some parents set very high standards for their teenagers making it clear, for instance, that kissing a date is to be left until engagement, and any more than holding hands and an occasional kiss is to be left until after marriage. These high standards may be reachable for their teenagers, but if the parents who are suggesting them did not reach these standards themselves, they need to be honest with their teenagers about their own behavior. Sometimes guilt feelings about their own behavior have led parents to set high standards for their teenagers. High parental standards are not the issue here as much as is the motivation for them.

When parents set high standards *for* their teenagers, they lose out on the thrill of pursuing standards *with* their teenagers. When parents dictate rules for their teenagers, they set themselves up for great satisfaction or for great heartache. If their teenagers live up to their standards, they can look back on their years as parents and brag "my teenagers lived up to my standards." But most parents who do this find their teenagers straining to be right on the edge of those standards, seeing how close they can get. Sometimes they drop over the edge.

When asked, "How far can we go?" parents might say, "How far do *you* think you should go? What kinds of dating activities will help you express affection for each other, and what kinds simply express physical passion?"

What a teenager decides about dating behavior will depend upon may things: his own self-image, his relationship with his parents, his relationship with God and the church, the type of friends he has, the age at which be begins dating, the degree to which he accepts the value system of his parents, and the degree to which he has developed his own values.

Because of the influence of the media, of friends, of too-young dating, the pressures on the dating scene, and just plain human nature, your teenager could find himself in a physical situation that is difficult to control. It is well to think and talk ahead of time about what is appropriate and right—how you look at a person of the opposite sex, how you touch and where, when and how you kiss, and the things that are never right in a dating experience. A young person should know what is reserved for marriage and know that it is in his best interest to save those actions and feelings for marriage.

Parents need to know what is accepted behavior among the majority of teens in their local high school, and among young people in their church. Some teens and young adults who draw the line before intercourse see petting and stimulation to orgasm as an alternative. But such actions work against trust in a future marriage relationship, and can produce guilt and lowered feelings of self-worth. Anything which works against oneself or a dating partner in any way cannot be considered within the will of God—or reflecting a Christian standard.

There is much laxity within the Christian world today and parents will do well not to assume anything. Each child needs the inner protection of positive self-image, of achievements, of a personal experience with God in Christ, of parental love and companionship, and of parental involvement in his life and interests. Add to these an adequate sex education by parents and church and school, and you will probably have a teenager who can date with confidence and pleasure, and treat others with the same respect that he feels for himself.

Once a teenager has decided with you what his or her behavior is going to be, the key question is, *"How* am I going to stick to this plan?" "How am I going to keep my relationship with my date and hold to my standards at the same time?" "How am I going to say No when I feel like saying Yes?" If you can guide your teenagers toward answers that satisfy them, you will have helped them in a most significant way.

Wright and Inmon suggest several things couples can do to avoid going beyond their intended limits. If your teenagers ask you for ideas, you might suggest one or more of these but keep the pressure on them to think creatively. The ideas they come up with are the ones that will probably work best for them.

1. I can pick my dates carefully. I deserve the best.
2. I can double or group date until I know the person I'm dating.
3. I can plan dates carefully in advance.
4. Finding out my date's ambitions in life is a way of affirming her or him as a person.
5. I can try my best to be consistent as a person and as a Christian, remembering Jesus lives in me.
6. I can talk with my date about my sexual ideals and standards, and my goals for a Christian home.
7. I can change the mood in any of several ways if I begin to get too turned on.
8. We can plan to be doing things while we talk and enjoy being together, minimizing "parking."
9. I can say NO!
10. Self-respect is more important than anybody's friendship.

Expectations

The expectations that a teenager's peers have for dating make setting and maintaining standards for sexual behavior increasingly difficult. Where dating used to be our culture's method of mate selection (meaning marriage), for some it has now become an end in itself, and for others, a method of finding a partner for sexual encounter (without commitments).

Most boys date with the expectation that they will go as far toward sexual intercourse as the girl will let them; she is responsible to stop progress. If she says "stop," boys expect to keep trying because she might just be "playing hard to get." This is such an assumed expectation that sometimes boys go further than they want to simply because they are afraid they will lose face if they do not keep pressing.

You can help your teenagers by questioning this expectation. Where 10 years ago a boy who didn't "go for it" was considered shy, polite, or maybe inhibited, now if he does not he is considered unusual, even weird! A very helpful aspect of sex education for early adolescents is to help them understand the world's expectations, and suggest that a mark of manliness and maturity is that a guy can take responsibility, set his standards, and communicate them to his date. Then he can be responsible to stop the progress of sexual intimacy.

Girls too have expectations, for themselves as well as for their dates. Boys are generally assumed to go as far as they can, and that the girls must stop progress. But many girls feel that they will not get a date unless they let the boy "have what he wants." This expectation makes saying No extremely difficult. A girl has much to lose either way—self-respect and maybe the respect of her boyfriend if she says Yes, and popularity, friendship, status, and immediate intimacy if she says No.

In the last few years the expectation has grown among young adults that the purpose of dating is sex. The disco scene has facilitated this idea tremendously. As young adults date older teenagers, and as they in turn date younger teens, this expectation is pervading the whole dating scene. Early conversations about dating, sexuality, standards for sexual behavior, marriage and its meaning, ways to plan dates, alternative dating experiences, etc., are imperative parts of sex education.

Values

One of the developmental tasks of teenagers is the rethinking of their values and the formation of their own value systems. A key determiner of the kind of moral values they will end up with is the value they place in themselves as young teens. Lawrence Kohlberg and other researchers have shown the tremendous weight teenagers place on the opinion significant other people have on their opinions.

Parents are usually still "significant others" to young teenagers. So as parents, you can help your teens value themselves much more if you invest hope, belief, love, affirmation, time, conversation, and responsibility in them. Then, for your teens, premarital sex may become something no self-respecting teenager would do.

9

Communication—Key to Your Teens

By the time your child has grown into the middle teen years, most of his or her pivotal attitudes and values toward sexuality will have been established. Ironically this is the age when many parents begin to become concerned about sex education and the age at which teenagers often reap the traumas that were sown by lack of sex education in earlier ages.

Teenagers are concerned about independence. An aspect of independence is the feeling of competence, intelligence, and being "with it." Naivete about any aspect of sexuality is threatening to most teenagers. So when they hear words they are not familiar with, ideas they've not been exposed to, or behaviors that surprise them, they are often left in a dilemma. If they ask the meaning of the word or idea, they expose their ignorance. If they don't ask, they are stuck with guessing and remaining ignorant until their guess is somehow confirmed or corrected. They often bluff each other, thus propagating considerable misinformation.

Parents can be of special help to teenagers in three important ways. First, parents can be resources for their teenagers, available to help them answer questions, form opinions and develop values and standards. Second, parents can be approachable. Even shy teenagers will discuss sexuality if parents are open. Third, parents can be understanding and forgiving when teenagers make mistakes. Their response can often preclude more mistakes.

Two very helpful resources for parents and teens need to be mentioned at this point. The one for parents is *Dating, Courtship, and Marriage* by Norman Wright and Marv Inmon. The other is *A Love Story* by Tim Stafford (Grand Rapids: Zondervan Publishing House, 1977). Wright and Inmon concentrate on the things parents can do to prepare their teenagers for marriage. Stafford focuses on answering teenagers' questions about sex, dating, and love.

Communication and Adolescent Issues

Conversations with teenagers can be natural, easy, and frequent if parents have been talking with them at their own levels during childhood. Of course, a talkative child may become a noncommunicative teenager. But the opposite often happens, too, as a tight-lipped child becomes a talkative teenager. The issue is more one of trust and openness than of talkativeness. If your teenager seems noncommunicative, you might read *Communication, Key to Your Teens* by Norman Wright and Rex Johnson (Irvine, California: Harvest House Publishers, 1978).

Two subjects that Christian teenagers wrestle with—and rarely get practical help for—are lust and masturbation. They may hear about lust and not really know what it means. Also helpful communication concerning masturbation is rare, especially in any kind of positive environment. Consider these two issues with the aim of learning to discuss them *with* your teenagers from a biblical perspective.

1. Lust. This is an often misunderstood and misused word. Four Hebrew and three Greek words are translated into the English word "lust" or "to lust after."

The Hebrew word *sheriruth,* translated "lust" in the King James Version, is more accurately translated "stubbornness, enmity or imagination."

Moses and the people of Israel sang a song of praise to God after their deliverance from Egypt: "The enemy said, 'I will pursue, I will overtake, I will divide the spoil; my desire shall be gratified against them; I will draw out my sword, my hand shall destroy them' " (Ex. 15:9). The word "desire" in the NASB is translated "lust" in other versions. It can also mean "soul" or "breath." Paraphrased, this verse might read, "I will get everything I want at their expense." This is the picture of pursuing soldiers anticipating rape. In this situation soldiers are not considering themselves as whole persons. They are playing their expected role of conquering fighters.

The word *nephesh,* translated "lust" or "desire" in Exodus 15 is also used in Psalm 78:18, but with no sexual connotation. "And in their heart they put God to the test by asking food according to their desire." The Israelites' problem was not one of hunger (a legitimate and often strong desire). God had provided food for these people. But they disdained His provision and demanded that God serve them from their own menu. Again, they forgot who they were as whole persons, God's persons, and focused upon their roles as gourmets.

Hedonism is an English word that comes from the Greek word *hedone* translated "lust" in James 4:1 and 3 in the King James Version. *Hedone* is better translated as "pleasures" in the NASB. In each instance in Scripture where the word *hedone* is used, whether translated "lust" or "pleasure," the emphasis is on gratification of natural or sinful desires. The word is related to the words *hedomai* (to be glad) and *hedeos* (gladly). The picture is one of gladness or happiness through gratification.

In Luke 8:14 it is the pleasures (hedone) of this life along with the worries and riches that choke the seed (the Word of God), preventing fruitfulness. In Titus 3:3, *hedone* and strong desires (lusts) are mentioned together as things which enslave a person. In each case the focus is gratification of a specific appetite, not a whole person acknowledging God-given needs, but treating a part of one's self as an object to satisfy. This kind of pleasure-seeking is never condoned in Scripture.

The question arises, then, "Is lust an action or a reaction?" Is it controllable or uncontrollable? Are the strong positive emotions a person experiences when seeing an attractive person of the opposite sex active or reactive? Is lust noticing someone attractive, that "second look," thinking twice about someone? Is lust flirting? Is it daydreaming about someone? Is masturbating, with someone in mind, lust?

The issue of "when lust begins" comes up in Matthew 5:27-28 where Jesus said, "You have heard that it was said, 'You shall not commit adultery'; but I say to you, that everyone who looks on a woman to lust for her has committed adultery with her already in his heart." Some people say these verses show that a man cannot help seeing an attractive woman, but he should not notice her. Others have said that it is the second glance or maybe the third or fourth that turns a look into lust.

If lust is a reaction, something uncontrollable like blinking, then a case might be made for equating a look or a second look with lust. But Jesus did not say that everyone who looks on a woman has committed adultery with her already in his heart. What He said was "that everyone who looks on a woman *to lust for her* has committed adultery with her already in his heart."

If lust is a fanning of desire, a catering to desires—even normal, God-given desires—if perspective is lost and God's design for sexual relationships based on mutual commitment is shunned, then lust is something controllable. If lust is an action rather than a reaction, I am responsible for it. I choose to lust or not to lust.

The phrase "to lust for her" in Matthew 5:28 gives the phrase "who looks on a woman" purpose. This purposefulness and responsibility is described in Romans 6:12-13. "Therefore do not let sin reign in your mortal body that you should obey its lusts (desires), and do not go on presenting the members of your body to sin as instruments of unrighteousness." Some desires are wrong and sinful and out of God's design for the expression of sexuality. If these desires are enhanced, entertained, and enriched by looking on another person's body, these desires control one's thoughts. This is what Christ equates with adultery, *if the other person is someone to whom you are not married.* If the object of your desire is your spouse there can be no adultery.

Second Peter 2:19 further clarifies the nature of lust and gives us a principle for discerning when lust is sinful and when it is not. ". . . for by what a man is overcome, by this he is enslaved." When desires, even strong ones, are acknowledged and kept within God's design for their expression, they are blessed and fruitful. But when we let our desires overcome us, we are enslaved. We can be overcome by entertaining our desires until as James 1:14 says, we are "carried away and enticed."

A second way to be overcome by desires is by denying their existence, in effect saying "I don't have any sinful desires any more; God has taken away my sinful nature." A person who denies desires in this way is burying them alive. They will eventually surface with overwhelming force.

Teenagers need to discuss this subject with their parents to avoid the confusion and guilt that is so common.

2. Masturbation. This is a subject on which there is a wide variety of opinion, not only in society at large, but also within the Christian church.

Following are two quotations presenting different approaches to the subject. Both men see that a problem exists, but don't confront it in the same way.

The first quote is by Dr. David Seamands, pastor of the United Methodist Church in Wilmore, Kentucky. His material has been used on occasion by representatives of Family Concern.

Although Menninger states that the taboo against masturbation vanished almost overnight at the turn of this century, the taboo about discussing it certainly did not.

Only in the past few decades have secular sources begun to write about it, while up-to-date Christian discussion has been limited to recent years. Secular psychologists and psychiatrists tend to confuse the issue by making the term too inclusive; so a simple definition is in order.

Masturbation is deliberate and conscious self-stimulation so as to produce sexual excitement with the goal of orgasm. Masturbation can be observed in small children, but the chief period for it is during adolescence and early young adulthood. Without doubt, it is the major sexual activity of teenagers.

There is no clear and direct word on masturbation anywhere in Scripture. When we know how almost universal and ancient masturbation is (it is mentioned in the *Egyptian Book of the Dead,* circa 1550-950 B.C.) and when every other sexual sin such as fornication, adultery, homosexuality, and bestiality are listed and clearly condemned, why is it—if it is always a sin—nowhere mentioned in the Bible? I realize the argument from silence is dangerous, but in the case of something so widespread and well known it would seem to be conspicuous by its absence.

From a scientific and medical standpoint we now know that there is no mental or physical harm in masturbating, so there are no moral arguments for health reasons. All this means that we will have to use other related Christian principles in determining its rightness or wrongness.

I believe the act of masturbation in itself is neither good nor evil. Two basic Christian principles determine this.

First, the thought life. When masturbation is accompanied by sexual fantasies it clearly comes under the condemnation of Christ's words about "mental adultery" in Matthew 5:27-28 and is a sin.

Second, the social and relational life. When masturbation, with or without lust, becomes an emotional substitute for proper interpersonal relationships, when it is used as a means of escaping from the pressures of loneliness, frustration, and depression, then there is no question that it is harmful to the person and therefore wrong from a Christian viewpoint.

Years of counseling have forced me to distinguish between masturbation as a temporary and occasional means of relieving normal sexual build-up (almost an inevitable part of normal growing up, particularly for teenage boys) and masturbation as a compulsive enslaving habit which feeds, and is in turn fed by, deeper emotional hang-ups. Some of these would include an inability to relate to any person—especially those of the opposite sex—depression, deep-seated resentments, and the inability to find normal ways of coping with frustration and anxiety. In this case masturbation is really only a symptom for deeper problems which are far more serious and damaging than it is. In my experience some of the worst cases of the latter kind are among married persons. Masturbation can, in a Christian, unfortunately become the peg upon which he hangs his guilts and anxieties that keep him from actually getting to the real problem. Parents, pastors, and Christian counselors must learn to discern the difference between the various types.

I have discovered the following to be some practical ways of dealing with masturbation:

1. Do not try a direct, frontal spiritual attack. Instead of lessening the problem, it usually makes it worse. Nothing provokes masturbation more than to create anxiety about it. Try to get the person's mind off his guilt and anxiety by explaining to him that it is one of those gray areas where rightness or wrongness depends on other factors.

Usually he has already tried prayer and Scripture reading, with the only result that he feels worse than ever for breaking his promises to God. His prayers are often doing more harm than good, for they are totally negative. Words of reassurance about God's accepting love, His faithfulness even when we fail and teaching the person how to pray positively ("Thank You, Lord, for loving me and healing me and helping me with all my problems") will help break the vicious circle of guilt and despair.

2. Get his mind onto his social life and his interpersonal relationships. Often he is a lone wolf and needs to break out of himself. "Socialize, don't fantasize" is another good suggestion. Persons who do this find within a matter of a few months that the compulsive nature of masturbation has been broken, reduced to a minor and only occasional means of relieving sexual tensions which finally may be abandoned altogether. The true joys of making friends, finding companionship, or of a dating relationship have filled the need

formerly filled by a poor substitute. He no longer mastur-
bates, because he doesn't need to. He has grown up, matured,
and "put away childish things."

When there is openness of communication on the subject of
sex, including masturbation, it will be simply an incidental
part of growing up and not become a major problem. As one
of my teenagers said to me one day when we were talking
about it, "Don't worry, Dad; it's sure no big deal with me!" I
think that sums up my view. It's high time we stop making
such a "big deal" out of masturbation and give it the well-
deserved unimportance it merits. ("Sex, Inside and Outside
of Marriage," *The Secrets of Our Sexuality,* Gary R. Collins,
ed., Waco, Texas: Word, Inc., 1976, pp. 151-156. Used by
permission of Word Books, Publisher, Waco, Texas 76703).

The second quotation is by Jack Wyrtzen, founder and co-
director of Word of Life, Schroon Lake, New York and his son,
Dave Wyrtzen, who is a pastor and doctoral candidate at Dallas
Theological Seminary.

Sex is one of the gods of the pagan American culture, and is
used to motivate people to buy movie tickets, brush their
teeth, and buy cars. Faced with this constant diet of sexual
stimulants, it is little wonder that masturbation is extremely
common in young men and women. The lack of explicit
reference to masturbation in Scripture, and the condoning
counsel of an increasing number of Christian leaders has left
young people unclear about the matter.

Is masturbation sinful? In order to answer this, we must
first clarify exactly what sin is. Sin in its most comprehensive
sense is anything that does not bring glory to God. Paul
wrote, "Whether, then, you eat or drink or whatever you do,
do all to the glory of God" (1 Cor. 10:31). We are made in the
image of God, and whatever we do is to express God's
character, purposes, and desires.

To answer our question about masturbation, we also need
to understand God's purpose and desire in giving sex to
mankind. Sex is presented in Scripture not only as a means of

populating the earth, but as a beautiful object lesson picturing the union between Christ and the church. As a man and a woman unite in the marriage act, two persons become one flesh. Human sexuality is to express a unity of mutual love, and unselfish sharing between two persons.

Self-stimulation of the sexual organs denies that God desires sex to be the expression of love and unity between two people. Masturbation is a selfish act to satisfy one's sexual needs. God's desire is that sex be an unselfish act to satisfy the need for love and intimacy in a marital partner.

God not only desires sex to be unselfish, but also desires that we control this drive. Much of the counsel justifying masturbation is based on the reality that young people have intense sexual drives. Because these drives cannot be met in marriage until schooling is completed, financial security achieved, masturbation is presented as a temporary release. I suspect that this advice is based on the frequently held assumption that suppression of any desires is bad. According to the slogan, "If it feels good, do it," the cure for pressing drives is to release them.

God's Word tell us, "All things are lawful for me, but I will not be mastered by anything" (1 Cor. 6:12). The New Testament warns us not to give in to the lusts of the flesh, specifically in the sexual area. (See Romans 13:13-14; 2 Corinthians 12:21; 2 Peter 2:2, 18). The lusts of the flesh are desires to satisfy needs in ways contrary to God's plan.

Giving in to lust does not bring freedom, but enslavement. Masturbation will not control the sex drive, but the sex drive may control the individual who frequently engages in it.

The true culprit in sexual sin is the thought life. When Jesus taught about the subject of adultery, He was talking as much about the inward consent of the heart as about the outward act. Paul Henry Gebhard, Director of Sex Research at Indiana University, writes, "The majority of males and females have fantasies of some sociosexual activity while they masturbate. The fantasy not infrequently involves idealized sexual partners and activities that the individual has not experienced and even might avoid in real life." (Encyclopedia Britannica "Sex and Sexuality.") We don't need a Ph.D. to tell us that masturbation is bedmate with an impure thought life.

If masturbation is not God's desire for controlling sexual pressure, what is the Christian young person to do? He needs to avoid watching illicit sex on TV, reading about it in novels and magazines, and joking about it with friends. Constant thinking about sex will fan the flames of desire into a burning lust. The believer also needs to stay away from situations in which masturbation is convenient.

The biblical cure for intense sexual desire is marriage. "If they do not have self-control, let them marry; for it is better to marry than to burn" (1 Cor. 7:9). As believers fall in love and their God-given sexual desire burns intensely, they are to marry to fulfill this desire. Until God provides a partner, His children are to allow the Spirit to control their sexual desires.

A young person may admit that masturbation does not glorify God and that marriage or self-control is the answer. But what about the reality of present enslavement to this habit? Jesus said, "If therefore the Son shall make you free, you shall be free indeed" (John 8:36). And the Apostle John reminds us that the "blood of Jesus Christ, His Son, cleanses us from all sin" (1 John 1:7).

If you are in bondage to this habit, talk to the Lord. Tell Him that you now recognize masturbation is sinful, and that it does not honor His purpose and desire for sex. Thank Him that the Lord Jesus died to forgive you and deliver you from all sin, this one being your need right now. Accept His forgiveness.

The risen Christ can deal with masturbation. When you are tempted, remember that this is one of the sins which put Christ on the cross. Recognize that God created a new person in you when you believed who can obey His desires, and rely upon the Spirit's power to overcome the temptation. "If you walk by the Holy Spirit's power you will not fulfill the desires of the flesh" (Gal. 5:16).

Remember, "And whatsoever you do in word and deed, do all in the name of the Lord Jesus, giving thanks to God and the Father by Him" (Col. 3:17). You can't masturbate in the name of Jesus, and thank the Father for it. It is a selfish perversion of God's unselfish sacred gift. Turn away from it, and rejoice in Christ's power to give you self-control over lust, and look forward to God's provision of a partner when you can use your sexual desires according to His glory!

When Trouble Comes

The best education in the world will not insure a person's success in any area of life. The best sex education parents can give will not insure a trouble-free growth through adolescence into adulthood and maybe marriage. So what can parents do when trouble strikes their family? How would you handle the situation if your teenage son told you his girlfriend was pregnant, and he was the father? Or what if your teenage daughter told you she was pregnant and wanted an abortion? Or if your son confessed that he was a homosexual. Or if your daughter, who wanted very much to be married, decided that the only way she could get attention from any man was to sacrifice her virginity.

Has sex education stopped when we are forced to confront one of these problems? No! If one of these situations happens in your family, you can view it in one of two ways—as a final exam which you just flunked, or as a challenge to forgiveness, concern, love, and healing. God is the model for parents in His relationship with His people.

How should you respond to your teens' behavior, when they have gone against all of your values and teaching? This question is especially important in the area of sexuality, because the consequences of sexual mistakes are so devastating.

Reaction interferes with positive action. When a teenager finally gets to the point of admitting a serious mistake to his parents, you know the point of desperation has been reached. Teenagers predict consequences on the basis of past experience. So if they have experienced punishment in the past when they have disobeyed, they will do almost anything to avoid that punishment again.

Take the dilemma of a 16-year-old who is pregnant. The romance and clandestine excitement of premarital sex have now been replaced by morning sickness and the realization that her life is forever changed. She figures that if she tells her parents about her problem they will explode and maybe kick her out of her home.

Her boyfriend is now strangely distant but keeps urging her to go to a clinic and "have the problem taken care of." She believes that abortion is murder but, as far as she knows, none of the people who preach against abortion have ever been in the fix she is. She finds out that she can have the abortion without her parents knowing about it.

What should she do? If she tells her parents about her problem she knows she will touch off an explosion in her home. If she does not tell them she figures she will be able to get back to normal life rather quickly. What she does not think about is the wall she will be building between herself and her parents.

Abortion is a common "solution" to premarital pregnancy. It is so available, convenient, and sanctioned by society now that it is an attractive alternative even for professing Christians, who find ways of rationalizing abortion by treating human fetuses as objects rather than as persons. But the legality of abortion doesn't make it morally right.

Since abortion is so freely available, there has been a decline in "shotgun weddings." Yet, having to get married because of pregnancy is still an alternative that is often taken. But basing a marriage on a mistake is not living out the intention of marriage, as given in Scripture. One of God's intentions for marriage is to show how He relates to His people; God certainly does not coerce us into establishing a relationship with Himself! Salvation is offered as a gift which is ours for the taking—or rejecting. A shotgun wedding insures marital problems such as resentment, jealousies, inability to trust, and often alienation. These are sometimes worked out over time, sometimes just tolerated, but are often the stuff divorces are made from.

Alienation is a third alternative "solution" to premarital pregnancy—and to other problems teenagers present to their parents. "No daughter of mine is going to live like that around here—get out! Go live with your boyfriend. I don't care!"

It is one thing for a teenager to choose to leave home. He can, like the prodigal son, choose to repent and come back. To be kicked out is another thing. Alienation is a poor way to making anything right.

Avoid blaming. Blaming teaches children to project their sins, mistakes, and problems onto others. Trying hard to find "who is to blame" avoids the reality that probably many people and factors contributed to the problem. A better way of facing a difficult situation is to ask, "What was my contribution to this?" As each person involved asks this question, everyone can take responsibility for resolving the problem together. It allows for shared responsibility and cooperation in resolution.

Focus on resolution. Working together as a family to handle the crises of sex-related problems and deal with long range resolutions of mistakes can be a healing aspect of family life. This is not to imply that resolving such problems is easy. It is likely to be agonizing and demand much sacrifice and pain. But sacrifice, pain, and agony are what the Cross was all about. Sin always exacts its toll.

But grace, forgiveness, and love lived out by parents to a son or daughter is a picture of redemption. A son or daughter may be able to see the reality of God's grace, forgiveness, and salvation only as they experience these attributes of God, through their parents, in a crisis situation.

10

A Wedding or a Marriage?

Weddings are important social events in almost every culture. Weddings bring to mind beautiful brides, wedding cakes, flowers, organ music, candles, and a reception with wedding cake, candy, punch, and sometimes even a full dinner. Then, in a shower of rice, the newlyweds drive off in a car decorated with crepe paper, tin cans, and a "just married" sign, and they live happily ever after.

Implicit in weddings are the assumptions that: (1) The couple is old enough to have made a decision to marry each other and to begin living together as husband and wife. (2) The couple is somehow prepared for marriage. (3) The couple is prepared for sexual as well as social unity.

All too often, all three of these assumptions are unwarranted. Not many brides or bridegrooms have seriously considered the person that they are marrying, in terms of alternative choices they might have made. Few couples get the benefit of good premarital counseling. Even with the information available about sexuality, very few couples go into marriage with a clear understanding about establishing a sexual relationship.

Extensive training is required for entry into a profession but very little time is spent preparing couples for this important area of life and happiness—marriage.

By 1970, many writers, ministers, professors, and counselors were calling for mandatory premarital counseling. In some states, premarital counseling is mandatory if one or both members of the couple are under 18 years of age. But in even these states little or nothing is said about what kind of counseling or how much is needed. More and more churches are requiring premarital counseling for any weddings performed by their pastors. But thousands of churches still pay little attention to this most vital ministry.

Rev. Robert Dulin, Jr. in his address at the Continental Congress on the family in 1975 said, "Pastors should refuse to sell the birthright of their ministry to nurture marriages for the pottage of conducting a wedding. The church's ministry is not to conduct weddings. Its ministry is to nurture marriages before marriage and during marriage. If couples cannot make a commitment to nurture their marriage prior to the event then the church should say, "we cannot have your marriage solemnized here!"

What preparation is your son or daughter going to have for marriage? If you church has a premarital counseling program that includes at least six sessions plus 20 to 30 hours of reading and listening to tapes, be thankful. Anything less than this is inadequate.

During the National Alliance for Family Life Research in 1973, 2,500 professional family life educators and marriage counselors were polled about the need to strengthen family life in North America. Sixty-six percent of them said that "churches are NOT doing an adequate job of promoting and maintaining family life as a contemporary concept." Ninety-three percent felt that young people are NOT receiving adequate preparation for marriage from their parents (H. Norman Wright, "A Report on American Family Life" in *Marriage and Family Enrichment Resource Manual.* Denver: Christian Marriage Enrichment, 1979 p. 1).

If your church does not have a premarital counseling ministry, why not? One reason may be that parents have not asked for it. You might want to talk to your pastor about premarital counseling in your church. If he objects that he does not have enough time for it, suggest that premarital counseling can be led by trained lay couples like yourself. This is now being done in many churches and training materials are available.

But if your church cannot or will not provide premarital counseling for your son or daughter, the responsibility falls back on your shoulders, Dad and Mom, to do everything that you can to invest in your son or daughter's marriage, not just their wedding.

The expectations young people have of their parents as they approach their weddings are really few and simple. But maybe these expectations need to be questioned. Maybe you can do more than is presently expected to help your son or your daughter not only have a great wedding, but establish a great marriage.

What does premarital counseling have to do with sex education? Plenty! First, sex is an important part of a newlywed couple's relationship. Where as full expression has been prohibited, now it is blessed. The emotional intimacy that will make greater physical intimacy in sexual intercourse possible is one of the major concerns of premarital counseling. If couples can work through questions of choice, differentness, expectations, goals, etc. before their wedding, they can establish an emotional intimacy that will be the foundation for great sexual intimacy. Without the emotional bond, sex will lose its intimacy and become just another way of gratifying physical appetites.

Enlarging the Family Circle

Parents *can* have great influence in the decisions their children make about marriage. Many parents feel that the last major impact they can have on their children's lives is in helping them in their decision on whom to marry. Without negating the importance of this, a far more important influence can be made in the area of preparation for marriage itself if parents focus on the how-to of building a successful and happy marriage.

Of course, this is a lifelong pattern which starts with the model that parents give their children in their own marriage. It continues through the sex education and the education in living that parents provide for their children as they grow up. But a very important aspect includes the final few months and weeks before the marriage begins. I call this "immediate marriage preparation."

The first aspect of immediate marriage preparation (and it is sometimes difficult) is the process of bringing into one's family the person that your son or daughter has chosen to marry. Until you can accept their marriage partner, you will find that you can have little if any influence on the preparations they make for marriage. On the other hand, if you can accept your son's or daughter's choice, you may have a tremendous influence on the marriage choices that are made.

Premarital Conversations

Beyond accepting, you need to really know the person who will be a future-in-law. In the past, dating may have been away from the family and you may not have had much opportunity to get acquainted. Now suggest to your daughter or son that you would like to get to know the person they have chosen as a partner and that some double dates for the four of you would be appropriate, to talk about their marriage.

If your son or daughter seems defensive about this idea, you can be patient, and find out why. Whatever their attitude, you need to use special tact, and also plan evenings that will be truly enjoyable.

Some couples may be ready for long conversations about their coming marriage. Parents need to be careful that immediate marriage preparation conversations take place *with* the couple, *not to* or *at* the couple. Dialogue is important. They need to hear themselves talk, to each other and to you, as much as they need to hear what you have to say.

Most of your immediate marriage preparation conversations should be with both the bride and the groom rather than with your child alone. They need to consider together the issues you will bring up, rather than individually. If you initiate conversations with one of them without the other being present, you will bring suspicion upon yourself in both of their minds, as they have a chance to talk about it later.

1. Reasons for marriage. After your son and his girlfriend have announced their plans to get married, ask them to go out to dinner with you and your wife. After some friendly conversation, and when you are well into your dinner, begin your conversation. Some premarital counseling techniques can work well for you. One of the things I like to ask couples is, "You both probably had several choices and you chose this specific person. What are some of the reasons that you chose this person rather than any of the other people?"

If I were asking these questions of my son and his fiancee, I would start with the comment that I am not giving them an exam. Because they are planning on marriage, I am interested in knowing why they have chosen each other. I would then turn to my son's fiancee and say something like this: "Since you are going to become a part of our family, I am interested in knowing what you see in my son that led you to chose him from among others you have dated to be your husband. Would you mind telling me?" After she had finished telling me her reasons, I would then turn to my son and say something like, "Son, you have chosen this lovely girl to be your wife, share with me why you have picked her, OK?"

As my son shared his reasons with us I would be listening specifically for several things. First, are his reasons for choosing her selfish? Reasons like: "She cooks well, she is a good-looker, she cuddles well, she wants to make me happy," are all ways of saying "I'm interested in having someone make me the happiest person in the world . . . in having someone meet my demands and cater to me delights." To have some of these reasons mixed in is natural, but if the total tenor of his response is that she can meet his needs and do it better than anyone else, you might suspect that his reasons for marriage are rather selfish.

If his reasons are more like: "I enjoy making her happy. I like to do things with her. I love her very much and I think she needs me. She responds to my affection. I enjoy giving things to her." you are moving toward other-centered reasons for a marriage. Hopefully, a couple will express a balance between self-centered and other-centered reasons.

Totally self-centered reasons might suggest to you that your son or his fiancee really wants a servant rather than a wife or husband. Totally other-centered reasons might suggest to you that your son wants to be a father to his wife rather than a husband, or that your son's fiancee wants to mother your son. They might also suggest that your son is denying to himself and to you some of the needs and desires that are natural at this stage of life. If this is so, they need to face the reality of their needs and desires.

If you hear the totally self-centered or the totally other-centered kinds of answers, your dinner together is not the time to confront them with their selfishness or personal needs. By coming down hard on them and suggesting that their reasons for choosing a marriage partner are inappropriate, you might scare them out of more conversations.

A better alternative is to ask more questions, like, "What attractive personality traits do you see in the other person? What are some things that the other person says or does that warn you that you are going to have some difficulties to overcome? Which of your other friends have some of the same qualities your fiancee has?"

As you listen to the responses, you may feel that they have no good reason for getting married, or at least don't know what their reasons are. But remember, maybe you didn't think through your reasons for marriage either at that age. Yet you and your wife have managed to develop a happy home for some years now. So don't make comments like, "You don't have very good reasons for getting married, do you?"

The task of answering your questions will, in itself, show your son and his fiancee that they may not have thought enough about why they are getting married. As much as anything else, one of your most important roles in a first conversation such as this is to suggest some ideas that your son and his fiancee, or your daughter and her fiance, will discuss together on their own.

Guilt over premarital sex is still one reason many couples get married. They feel that they have done something they were not suppose to do and now they have to get married. This factor is not likely to come up in a dinner conversation, if it has not arisen before. However before the conversation is over, you might mention that one of your concerns is that they do not feel pressured into getting married. Two wrongs do not make a right.

Even when premarital sex is not involved, many couples feel pressured into marriage if they have dated for some time. People expect them to marry and the couple may have difficulty admitting that this is not what they want. Also, one member of the couple may feel pressured by the needs or dependence of the other and mistake a clinging vine or leaning tower need for love.

When a couple approaches marriage because of premarital sex or pregnancy, they need to rethink their plans. Mention that you are not saying this because you suspect their behavior, but because in our culture premarital sex is common and guilt is not a good foundation for marriage. If your son and his fiancee admit that this is one of the considerations in their decision to get married, avoid condemning them. Rather, work with them to rethink whether or not a marriage started on the basis of guilt and necessity is really the kind of relationship they want to establish. Maybe they would choose later to marry each other anyway, but they need to make sure that they are marrying because they love each other and want to establish a home together.

2. Expectations. A topic for a second conversation, and maybe even another dinner, is the subject of expectation. What does each expect of marriage and of the other person as a spouse?

Expectations are a natural part of looking toward the future and a couple about to get married have many. Your objective in this conversation is to help them verbalize expectations they maybe didn't even realize. Here Dad might work with the groom and Mom with the bride asking them to list at least 25 expectations they have of the other person. As much as possible, avoid suggesting expectations. A list of 25 is not really very long.

When they have completed their lists, before they discuss their expectations with each other, start with the first expectation and ask your son how he will respond if his fiancee does not live up to it. Have your wife ask the same question of your son's fiancee. Proceed through each of the expectations they have listed, talking about how they will respond in each case if that expectation is not realized in the life of the other person. As they share what their response will be, jot down notes for each expectation so you have a record of the kind of responses your son and his fiancee are giving.

If they do not list anything in the area of sex, you might ask them to talk about these expectations too. Their reluctance to list them might indicate some fear or some reluctance to be involved in sex, or misunderstanding of each other's expectations, or embarrassment in front of you. To help them, you might share what your expectations were for sexual closeness when you were first married and how these were realized or not realized. Be sure to share how you coped with those that were not realized.

Talking about sex openly with your children is important, because it will give them the freedom to come to you after they are married, if they have difficulties with sex. If they don't feel free to talk to anyone, they could endure needless difficulties for a long time. Sexuality is so important that it is worth a whole evening's conversation by itself. I will suggest how to go about it shortly.

Now ask them whether each expectation is easy to realize or difficult. Some expectations will probably be difficult. They may have to change their behavior to meet each other's needs. This needs to be discussed. What kinds of changes will be made? Are those changes fair to expect? How will a person cope if the other doesn't change?

3. *Differentness.* A third marriage preparation conversation might revolve around the area of differentness and similarity. When two families are united by marriage, two sets of customs and ideas about family interaction come together. For instance, one family's response to conflict is to sit down and talk immediately, whereas in another family conflict is something that is denied. In one family a person may yell when he gets angry, swear, and say all sorts of things he does not really mean. In another family, anger is not expressed that way—they only say what they mean and mean what they say.

So if a couple marries, not having worked through these areas of differentness, they may be surprised by the other person's behavior and find it difficult to understand. Each person has different ideas that he has learned from his parents about how to live in a family. At marriage, these different ideas often clash. Sometimes the little things cause the problems because little things tend to mount with other little things to the point that they become a big problem that needs to be discussed. But neither member of the marriage team knows where to start.

At your third meeting, start a conversation about differentness by suggesting some of the things that you do in your family that you suspect are different from other families. Then ask your son's or daughter's fiance if that is the way that they do the same thing in their family. Try to list as many ways as you can that your family is different from theirs. If the couple brings humor into these differences, it is a healthy sign that your son and his fiancee can adapt to each other. Danger to a marriage comes when one family's way of doing something is presumed to be "the right way," and another family's way wrong.

Make this conversation fun as you explore the new family patterns made possible by two families coming together. But make sure that your son and his fiancee have had the opportunity to think through how they will respond to each other's differentness. The tendency is to try to turn the other person into a photocopy of one's self. The choice to change, in order to accommodate to the other person's values, habits, and behaviors, shows a healthy, mature response.

4. Goals and finances. A fourth topic concerns the goals a young couple have as they begin their marriage. Where do they want to be in five years? What do they want to be doing in a year that will help them arrive at where they want to be in five years? What are some of the things that they want from the first three or four months of their marriage? You might start by asking them each to list five goals they have for marriage, one goal they have for themselves, and one goal they have for each other.

Then ask them these questions: (1) How did you arrive at these goals? Are they from your parents, your church, society, or friends? (2) Which are your most important goals? Which goal or goals could you do without, if absolutely necessary? (3) Which goals are going to take money? (4) Which goals do you feel God considers important? (5) What are some things you are going to do to reach those goals?

The rest of your conversation can center around thinking through a budget. What is their income going to be each month? What are their expenditures? So many couples have an unrealistic idea of the income necessary just to live. Try to help them come up with a workable budget.

5. Sexuality. A fifth topic for conversation in immediate marriage preparation is sexuality. This is often an uncomfortable subject for conversation both for parents and for the couple. One of the best ways to deal with this topic is to listen to the tapes by Dr. Ed Wheat, *Sex Problems and Sex Techniques in Marriage.* Many counselors use these tapes in marriage counseling by sending them with the couple on their honeymoon. The danger of using them in premarital counseling is that a couple plays the tapes in their car cassette player as they are parked someplace together overlooking the lights of the city at midnight. The temptation to practice some of the techniques Dr. Wheat suggests is almost irresistible under these circumstances.

It is better to listen to the tapes together—that means you and the couple, and maybe your son's fiancee's parents as well. After you listen to them, you can discuss the concepts that Dr. Wheat shares. In premarital counseling I have had several couples listen to the tapes in this way and have found that, far from being embarrassing, these tapes can form the basis for more than one conversation. This is sex education at its best.

6. Other Conversations. The possibilities for conversations in immediate marriage preparation are many. You may want to talk about how they relate to each other when they are angry, or about conflict resolution. You can deal with the area of communication. You may even want to discuss children, parenting, and preparing for sex education for your grandchildren. Since the possibilities are so many, take care that you make your conversations count in the areas that are most important to the bride and groom. Do your best to deal with the questions they bring up. When you do not have answers, you can surely find some Christian books that will.

After the Honeymoon
If you have been involved in a healthy marriage preparation with your children, after the wedding and honeymoon you will probably have the privilege of talking with them more about their relationship. The investment that you make premaritally is worth the time if it opens doors for conversation after marriage.

11

Does Single Make It Different?

When divorce or the death of a parent comes to a family, many aspects of family life must change. Must sex education change? The obvious first answer is "Yes, of course." Now one parent is not there on a regular basis. Some mothers just do not feel comfortable about discussing matters of sexuality with their sons. Nor do some fathers want to talk about it with their daughters. But this does not mean that it can't happen.

Single parents can have healthy attitudes about sexuality, even if their experience in sex with their spouse has been frustrating. As they develop a healthy family atmosphere for sex education, they can talk with their children of either sex explicitly about sexuality, including the biological and functional aspects, as well as their values and feelings. Single parents can ask the same questions of their children and give the same answers that parents who are together can.

I believe that the single parent can also do well in premarital conversation. In fact, he or she may bring to the counseling situation a very helpful perspective that a couple could not.

Sex education is an opportunity for single parents to grow. It can either be welcomed or dreaded. The key issue for single parents is whether they have worked through their own feelings about sexuality. A review of the questions raised in chapter 2 will be helpful at this point.

But other issues may come up as a result of the re-forming of a family after divorce or death. Relationships change especially between mother and son, and between father and daughter. There is a need to work through grief or the problems that led to a divorce. New roles are forced upon everyone by the death or divorce. These matters need to be brought to a healthy resolution, or they will negatively affect attempts at sex education.

You Feel Inadequate?

Many married couples let sex education go unattended because they feel sexually inadequate themselves. This can be even more true for single parents, and also for a parent whose marriage is unhappy. The Christian single parent, lacking a relationship in which to express sexuality, may become quite uncomfortable talking about it even with his or her own children. Questions are asked, memories relived, or issues raised that remind a parent that he or she failed to establish the kind of relationship that might have prevented divorce. For those who lost a partner through death, the memories that come as a result of discussing sexuality may provoke grief again. Is a child of divorced or widowed parents, then, going to miss the opportunity for parental sex education?

Single parents love their children and want the best for them, as much as married parents do. So a better response than procrastinating on sex education or giving the responsibility to someone else who may not actually do it, would be for a single parent to approach the problem. For both the divorced and the widowed parent, this means working all the way through the grief process. For the divorced parent it means dealing with the problems that contributed to the divorce as well as those that have arisen since.

If you need help to do this, you may wish to work with a competent Christian counselor and some Christians in your church who are trained. It is important that conflicts be resolved—for your children's benefit as well as your own. With the right kind of help, you can come to the place where you are comfortable again in conversations about sexuality with your kids.

New Roles

I travel to weekend seminars periodically and when leaving, usually say to my seven-year-old son something like, "You're the man of the house while Daddy's gone. Take care of your mother and sisters!" Matthew bravely assumes his new role, at least until he is back from the airport. But children whose parents are widowed or divorced do not have the luxury of knowing Daddy will be back in two days.

Instead of a parting parent saying, "Take care of Mommy, or Daddy," the parent the child is living with often issues an unspoken demand, "Take care of me." New chores, fewer privileges, and greater responsibilities are often part of the new roles the children of a widow or divorced parent have to assume.

Because of the added responsibility, single parents may assume the children are more competent and prepared for life than they really are. Since children have faced the challenge of their new roles, the parents assume that they were quite competent and prepared all along. Their ability was just called for by the divorce or death.

But coping with parental death or divorce does not mean that kids are ready to deal with all other aspects of life they will face. They have coped, but not without anxiety. As they are faced with puberty, sexual pressure from their peers, questions about masturbation, lust, abortion, etc., they will probably cope again, but not without much needless anxiety.

The importance of open communication between parent and child cannot be overstated, especially for those facing new roles. Being open and honest about the new roles, our feelings about them—our need to periodically abandon them and revert to previous, more comfortable roles—will make coping and even growth possible.

Intimacy

In chapter 1, I quoted an anthropologist who pointed out that there are three distinct ways in which the design for living is learned: direct education of schooling, deliberate observation and imitation, and unconscious imitation or absorption. Since intimacy is such a large factor in sexuality and therefore in sex education, a single parent must remember that intimacy is more absorbed and imitated than taught directly. So how are children in one-parent homes going to learn intimacy?

Intimacy is such a vital part of sexuality that it is a major issue for sex education. Giving up on intimacy after a divorce or the death of a spouse is easy because intimacy may revive feelings that are too painful to be faced. So how is a single parent to teach his or her children the intimacy they will need to develop their own loving relationships?

First, understand that intimacy may be of several kinds. Intellectual intimacy is the feeling that you know what people are going to say before they say it. It is the fun of thinking and working together. It is what you hope for when working on a church committee with people you respect.

Physical intimacy is the freedom to touch one another, see one another, to let other people into your "life space." In marriage, physical intimacy is also sexual. God has made us with a need for total intimacy within marriage. When spouses cannot be emotionally or intellectually intimate, this affects physical intimacy adversely.

Emotional intimacy is the ability to touch one another emotionally. It is the ability to feel the pain another person is feeling as well as his or her joy. It takes communication, acceptance, openness, and honesty. It is a vital part of a growing marriage as well as a mark of personal maturity. Emotional intimacy is available even when physical intimacy is not. The notion that you can only be intimate with somebody with whom you are physically intimate is not true. And although physical intimacy helps emotional intimacy, the latter is not dependent upon it. In fact, the person looking for emotional intimacy through episodes of physical intimacy will find great disappointment.

You can build the capacity for emotional intimacy in your children even though your spouse is not present. A person grows in emotional intimacy; it is not something you "fall into." Nor is it something that can be experienced deeply all of the time. People just cannot live on an emotionally deep level constantly. It is too exhausting. Everyone goes to depths of intimacy periodically and comes back up. For this process to happen naturally, two things are needed—attention and freedom. To learn intimacy, a child must get attention from his parent or parents and must feel free to come and go emotionally.

To give a child this kind of freedom, a parent needs to be able to accept the child and to empathize with him. It is natural for children to feel emotionally close to parents sometimes and quite distant at other times. It is important for a parent to accept both the times when a child is feeling close and when he is naturally feeling distant. If a parent can *feel with* a child in both of those times, the relationship will become natural and flowing.

The character trait that kills naturalness in relationships is possessiveness. If, as a single parent, you tend to possess your children and make them dependent, you will kill their naturalness in intimacy. Adults can feel more intimate with each other when they see each other as equals and independent of each other. Children do not see themselves as equal with their parents or independent of them, in many respects, until they themselves are adults. But they *can* learn intimacy as they sense that their parents *trust* them, and as they gain independence as a result of that trust.

A final important aspect of developing intimacy is *honesty*. Everyone feels closer to people who can admit mistakes and problems. Anyone is afraid to be intimate with someone who is perfect. Sometimes parents portray themselves to their children as perfect, never admitting mistakes. This kind of dishonesty alienates. For children to learn or absorb intimacy from their parents and to develop the ability of emotional intimacy as an aspect of their sex education, parents must be growing in these qualities. Do you give attention and freedom to your children? Do you accept your children and empathize with them? Do you try not to possess them, but trust them and give them independence? Most important of all, are you honest with them?

You can continue to build an emotionally intimate home even though your children miss the modeling of physical intimacy they would have if your spouse were present. Your investment in their growth in emotional intimacy will aid greatly in the development of healthy attitudes toward their sexuality.

Study the Bible together to discover its answers to questions that come as children grow. Doing so is a foundational period of sex education. When the questions they ask turn to sexuality, you will have established a pattern for finding answers in the Bible.

Redefining Family

People are so used to the idea of a family being comprised of father, mother, and children that when death or divorce strike, they tend to think the family has been destroyed. But to say it has been destroyed is to give children the impression that they are on their own. They may respond to this message and act out their loneliness against the parent they are living with.

They still have family—parents, brother, sister perhaps, but they are not all under the same roof. This means that children need to learn to think of family more in terms of person-to-person relationships, rather than in terms of everyone together.

I believe redefining a family in terms of a larger whole—God's family—would be better yet. "I'm so glad that I'm a part of the family of God." The words of this popular Christian song give the picture of the kind of relationships that are available in the body of Christ, "God's forever family." First Peter 2:9 calls Christians "a chosen race, a royal priesthood, a holy nation, a people for God's own possession." Throughout the New Testament epistles Paul called the people of God "brethren." A local church that actualizes these descriptions of the body of Christ will find ways to care for each other and build one another up, allowing each member to sense his part in the family.

Larry Richards writes, "Family members, as individuals and in all their family roles, have a tremendous need for support by the local body. . . . With the contemporary strain placed on the nuclear family by such factors as rapid pace of change, the pluralization of society, and the distribution of functions that were once the family's to other units of society, for family members and family units to receive support from the local church is all the more vital."

Two of the implications Richards sees in this imperative are: (1) "The local church must accept responsibility to minister to and support believers 'in family' and to help individuals fulfill vital family roles." (2) "Families need support as units, with specific help given to develop a relational climate that makes it possible for ministries to flow two ways within each family unit" (*How the Church Can Help the Family Face the Future,* Family Concern, 1976, pp. 2-3).

Probably the members of the body of Christ who need this kind of family support most are those whose nuclear family is in some way disrupted. Single parents, for instance, and the children of divorced or widowed parents have a great need to be supported by their larger family—the family of God. One of the areas of support for single parents and children of divorced parents is that of sex education.

In a home where mother and father are both present, if the mother feels self-conscious about discussing sex education with her son she can defer to his father to instruct his boys while she does all of the sex education instruction with her daughters.

In a single-parent family this is not possible. A single parent's choice is usually limited. Either he or she is the children's teacher in sex education or they are left to get it for themselves from peers at school. The situation is further compounded by the sense of failure in sexuality that pervades many single-parent homes. The feeling that had they been successful in sexuality they might not have divorced will certainly inhibit a single parent from the free and easy discussion of sexuality that makes sex education in the home a positive and healthy dialogue.

Unfortunately, rather than giving a single parent those aspects of family life, many evangelical churches still alienate the single parent, especially the divorcee. And this is not likely to change—at least not immediately. What, then, can a single parent do to redefine family in a resistant, local congregation?

Options for Single Parents

Obviously one option is to move to another local church. At least these people will not be as likely to be aware of the problems that led to your being a single parent. But is this option running away from an opportunity to grow? Maybe it isn't. Maybe the only place you can feel free to grow is in a different group. But maybe it is running away. What about your children? They may need the friends they have right now instead of forming new friendships.

A second option is to establish a new extended family with one or more families in your church. You have wanted this but nobody has offered to extend their family to you. Biblical fellowship is a two-way process that begins with your initiative to build up another person or another family. The result, then, is that you are built up in turn. The home Bible study or growth group movement that has developed in recent years gives the promise of meeting some special need you may have as a single parent. The emphasis in these groups on fellowship and commitment may allow you to become comfortable enough with other members of the group that they can help you in the sex education task you have with your children. For instance, some members of the group might be able to answer questions you felt you could not honestly handle with your children.

Remember, sex education is much more than just giving your children the facts concerning their anatomy and physiology. Developing positive values and attitudes is probably the most important aspect of sex education in the long run. So get help as you need it—that is what being in the body of Christ is all about. One kind of help you can get in your congregation is that of several role models for your children to watch.

The Problem of Modeling

One of the assumptions underlying this whole book is the importance of the model that parents are to their children for sex education. Obviously if you are a single parent, the marriage model is missing. Married people often provide less than adequate models too. For instance, if children watch Dad treat Mom as if she were his servant, they will need another model for manly interaction with a woman.

How do you handle attitudes, behaviors, and values that are being consciously or unconsciously absorbed from interactions with your spouse when you feel that he or she is a faulty model for your children? First, be sure that your behavior is healthy and mature. Beware of going overboard in response to your spouse's problems and modeling behavior so opposite to his or hers that your behavior becomes immature.

Second, find and expose your children to models in your church who will help them in their growth and maturity. This is one of the important benefits of being a part of the church—the family of God.

Third, for you to ignore your spouse's immature behavior as much as possible is more helpful to your children than a frontal assault on it. Even young children are very perceptive of relationships. If they sense a security in your continued giving of love, they are much more likely to respond positively to you than if they see wedges being driven into their feelings toward the other parent by your constant frontal attack.

In Summary
Even though your marriage may not have survived, or you are widowed, or if you are in an unhappy relationship, you can still value Christian marriages as pictures of God's relationship to His people. And your home *can* be similar to this as you and your children learn about God and His relationship to His people, by experiencing the fellowship of the family of God as it functions biblically. But you may have to initiate this fellowship, first with one family in the church, then with others as they catch on.

The emotional intimacy you establish and work hard to develop with God's people and with your children will do much to prepare them for later emotional and sexual intimacy in their own marriages. This is truly healthy sex education.

12

Resources for Sex Education

As you read through the book, at some points you probably said, "I wish he had written more on this particular topic." In this chapter I hope to acquaint you with some of the best resources that are available so that you can obtain further information if you want it. This is not an exhaustive list and I will certainly miss some good books.

My comments on the purpose and approach of each book will give you an idea of what to look for. After the first title, the books are listed by the chapter to which they most apply.

Lewis P. Bird, and Christopher T. Reilly, *Learning to Love, A Guide to Sex Education Through the Church.* (Waco, Texas: Word, Inc. 1971) 182 pages. This book is in two parts. First, a Christian philosophy of sex education, and second, programs and problems. These include junior and senior high courses in sex education. It also suggests a course for parents. Appendix A contains a thorough list of sex education materials, resources, and books up to 1970.

Chapter 1
Lawrence O. Richards, *A Theology of Christian Education,* Grand Rapids: (Zondervan Publishing House, 1975) 324 pages. An in-

depth look at total life as an educational process, including what the church and families can do to help children, youth, and adults in this process. In his chapter on home as a nurture center, Richards writes, "The critical location for Bible teaching is not the classroom but rather the household—the walk, the sitting together on the porch, the snuggling into the warmth of bed, the joy of rising to a new day. It is in life itself, where Bible truths are to have meaning for us as whole persons, that their communications must center." From this perspective Richards gives many practical approaches to making a home the center of spiritual nurture.

B.A. Clendinning, Jr., ed. *Family Ministry in Today's Chruch,* (Convention Press, 1971) 139 pages. An excellent call to family ministry, this book starts with a biblical perspective. "The philosophical stance for an emphasis on family ministry must be firmly based on a biblical view on marriage and the family. This view . . . emphasizes the sanctity and permanence of marriage, the dignity and worth of person, the need for order and authority in family living, and the responsibility of the home for inculcating moral and spiritual values."

In discussing a Christian view of sex, Clendinning writes, "A home where love abounds is the ideal setting for teaching a Christian interpretation of sex, and trained parents are the logical teachers. The teaching of certain facts is the easy part of this instruction. Far more crucial are the attitudes that parents themselves have toward sex. . . . In few areas can home and church work together more effectively or to greater mutual advantage than in teaching both parents and children a Christian interpretation of sex." This book would be an excellent resource for a group or person planning family ministries in today's church.

Beatrice Braden, *Sex Was More Fun When,* (Los Angeles: Price, Stern, Slone, 1973). This short, humorous book highlights some of the misconceptions that arise from a lack of good sex education. This is not a Christian book, and does not attempt to solve miseducation issues—just to raise them in a humorous way.

Wesley Haystead, *You Can't Begin Too Soon,* (Regal Books, Glendale, Calif. 1974) 130 pages. This excellent book is not about sex education, but rather about helping little children to learn. Chapter 1, "The Child and Christian Concepts," is particularly helpful as Haystead writes about how a child thinks. The epilogue titled "Learning That Makes a Difference" gives excellent insight into talking with little children, asking them questions, building relationships, repetition, and other aspects of helping them learn.

Clair H. Amstutz, *Growing Up to Love: A Guide to Sex Education for Parents* (Scottdale, Penn. Herald Press, 1966).

Child Study Association of America, *What to Tell Your Children about Sex,* (Des Moines: Meredith Corporation, 1964).

Chapter 2

Of the many resources on sex, the ones listed are specially helpful in the area of attitudes toward sex and a theology of sexuality.

Harry Hollis, Jr., *Thank God for Sex. A Christian Model for Sexual Understanding and Behavior,* (Nashville: Broadman Press, 1975) 167 pages.

> "Lord, some people say
>   sex and religion don't mix;
> But Your Word says sex is good.
> Help me to keep it good in my life.
> Help me to be open about sex
>   And still protect its mystery.
> Help me to see that sex
>   Is neither demon nor deity.
> Help me not to climb into a fantasy world
>   Of imaginary sexual partners;
> Keep me in the real world
>   To love the people you have created.
> Teach me that my soul does not have to frown at sex
>   For me to be a Christian."

Hollis begins each chapter with a poetic prayer. His book is a theology of sexuality and deals with issues such as "The Good

News about Sex," "The Model," "Biblical Teachings," "The Contemporary Smorgasbord," "God's Creative Activity," "The Purposes of Intercourse and Marriage," "Responding to God's Creative Activity," "Sex and Self-discipline," "Sex and Love," "Communicating about Sex through the Church," "The Church and the Future of Sex."

Lewis B. Smedes, *Sex for Christians. The Limits and Liberties of Sexual Living,* (Grand Rapids: Eerdmans, 1976) 250 pages. To quote from the cover, "While the Bible does not spell out the detailed theory of sex, it does open up for us a perspective on life as a whole, including our sexuality. Our bodies must be seen as part of the glory of creation which God called good and which He redeemed in Jesus Christ. We are to rejoice in the rich possibility that they offer for enjoyment and communion. . . . Smedes also addresses frankly but sympathetically, such matters as erotic fantasies, homosexuality, and mere sensualism.

"*Sex for Christians* offers a throughly contemporary, unprudish, but solid biblical look at a subject of intense concern to Christians today."

Dennis Guernsey, *Thoroughly Married,* (Word, 1975) 145 pages. "It's my deepest conviction that genuinely liberated Christians will have the best and sexiest marriages if they really take hold of the freedom Jesus gives." *Thoroughly Married* offers help for Christian couples to break through barriers to more honest communication, learn how to handle anger in constructive ways, enrich their marriage through a mutual understanding, gain freedom to be spontaneous and creative in love-making, and enjoy sex as a beautiful natural gift from God. Even the first chapter is worth the price of this book. In it Dr. Gurnsey shows from 1 John 3:16-18 what it is to become a lover.

Other chapter titles include: "Preparing Your Marriage for Love-Making," "Preparing Your Wife for Love-Making," "Preparing Your Husband for Love-Making," "Understanding Your Wife's Sexuality," "Understanding Your Husband's Sexuality," "Free to Enjoy Your Sexuality," and "When There Are Problems." "Most of all I would encourage each of you to think in terms of tasting all that God has meant for you to enjoy as a special part of His creation. Nowhere is His creation more enjoyable than the one-flesh relationship of marriage. When each of us is all that we were meant to be then we are truly free indeed."

Ed Wheat, M.D. and Gaye Wheat, *Intended for Pleasure, Sex Technique and Sexual Fulfillment in Christian Marriage.* (Old Tappan, N.J., Revell, 1977) 223 pages. To quote from the cover, "This book has been written for every married or soon-to-be married person who is searching for a medically accurate presentation of sex in marriage within the framework of the Bible's teaching. It is sure to become a standard reference volume and valuable in homes where children receive sex education based on biblical principles. The Wheats apply what the Bible has to say about sex to our everyday life in a meaningful way. After all, God Himself invented sex for procreation and delight. It was His gift to us intended for pleasure."

Chapter titles include "Understanding the Basics," "One Flesh: The Techniques of Love-Making," "Solutions to Common Problems," "For the Pre-orgasmic Wife: Fulfillment Ahead," "For the Impotent Husband: Fulfillment Again," "Planning and Achieving Parenthood," "Sex Techniques during Pregnancy," "Sex After 60, 70, 80," and "Answers to Your Questions." The final chapter, titled "Your Marriage: A Private Little Kingdom," in a beautiful way points couples to better relationships with each other and to establish and develop a personal relationship with God.

Ed Wheat, M.D., "Sex Techniques and Sex Problems in Marriage," cassette tapes available from Scriptural Counsel, Inc., Dept. D, 130 Spring, Springdale, Ark. 72764. In the pamphlet which comes with the cassette, Dr. Wheat writes, "Several years ago my wife Gaye and I became personally concerned with the need to provide a medically accurate presentation of sex in marriage from the viewpoint of the Bible-believing Christian. The result is this set of cassettes which are designed to answer the questions Christian couples are asking about sexual fulfillment. The subject is treated as the Bible treats it. Openly, factually, and yet reverently, for we are speaking of God's sacred plan for marriage."

These tapes are especially helpful in premarital and marital counseling. I mention them here because many people who are experiencing sex problems in marriage are not readers but can find practical help from listening to these cassettes.

H. Norman Wright, "Sex and the Bible," a cassette two-pack available from Probe Media, Inc., 17975 Sky Park Blvd., Suite E, Irvine, California 92707. The first of these two tapes goes into the reasons for discussing the Scriptures and sex, some basic principles for sex education and an overview of the Old and New Testament teaching—what the Scripture teaches about sex for pleasure and sex play, what the Scripture says about fornication, adultery, prostitution, homosexuality, masturbation, incest, rape, bestiality, and lustful thoughts.

Dwight Hervey Small, *Christian: Celebrate Your Sexuality* (Revell, 1974)

Helmut Thielicke, *The Ethics of Sex* (Grand Rapids: Baker Book House, 1975)

Roy W. Fairchild, *Christians in Families* (Chicago: Covenant Press, 1964)

Chapter 3

Rex Johnson and H. Norman Wright, *Building Positive Parent-Teen Relationships,* (Irvine, Calif. Harvest House Publishers, 1978) 79 pages. This is a teaching guide including transparencies and duplicating patterns. Session 2 is titled "Styles of Home Atmosphere," and delineates both negative and positive styles of home atmosphere. Although not specifically related to sex education, it further clarifies the content of chapter 3 in this book. Session 3 in *Building Positive Parent-Teen Relationships* is titled, "A Christian Home or A Home Full of Christians." It is a study of the implications of Romans 5:1-5. The objective of both of these sessions is to help a family develop a truly Christian family atmosphere.

Chapter 4

Ed Reed and Bobbie Reed, *Creative Bible Learning for Youth,* (Regal, 1977) 190 pages. This is a book about Bible learning in the Sunday School. In chapter 2 titled, "What Youth Need to Grow," the Reeds discuss several factors in learning responsibility, including growing to sexuality and single relationships, growing to self-identity and love, growing to independency and self-discipline, and growing to a value system and relationship with God. The suggestions they give for teachers are also excellent for parent-teachers as you instruct your children at home.

Chapter 5

H. Norman Wright, *Communication—Key to Your Marriage,* (Regal, 1974) 194 pages. This book is a must for Christian couples. It not only talks about communication but helps couples communicate. A married couple who cannot communicate with each other has little hope of establishing the healthy communication patterns with children that are necessary for good sex education. So here is a start.

Some of the chapters include "What Was That I Never Heard You Say?" "Why Can't We Talk About It?" "How to Handle Anger Before It Handles You," "How to Cope with Conflict," "Communicate to Build Self-esteem." To quote from the foreword: "One of the best things about this book is that it's more than a book. It's an experience in learning, caring, and communicating. You don't simply read this book, you dialogue with it—and hopefully, with your partner. You don't just talk about communicating. You *do* it—perhaps for the first time."

Thomas Gordon, *Parent Effectiveness Training,* (P.H. Widen, 1970) 338 pages. P.E.T. has become a widely known book since its publishing in 1970. Christians will not agree with all of Gordon's philosophy of parenting, but he gives many practical means of establishing, developing, and maintaining communication with children of all ages.

Norman Wright and Rex Johnson, *Communication—Key to Your Teens,* (Harvest House, 1978) 157 pages. And Rex Johnson,

Communication—Key to Your Parents, (Harvest House, 1978) 144 pages. The teenage years seem to be the time when many communication problems become apparent. These books deal with coping with those problems, reestablishing relationships that may be torn, and enriching relationships that still exist. While the focus of these books is not sexuality, they both contain chapters that deal with the issues for teenagers. For instance, Dressing, Driving, Dialing, and Dating is one chapter title in each book, taking the same issues from parent and teen perspectives.

Sven Wahlroos, *Family Communication,* (New York: Macmillan Publishing Co., 1974)

John Gottman, *A Couple's Guide to Communication,* (Champaign, Ill: Research Press, 1976).

Chapters 6 and 7

Helen I. Driver, Ed., *Sex Guidance for Your Child,* (Madison, Wis: Monona-Driver Book Co., 1960) 192 pages. This excellent secular book includes background information, descriptions of responsibilities of parents, of school, of the church, of parent study groups. In part two, the authors discuss specific problems and questions, including infancy and the preschool years. Some of the topics discussed in chapter 10 are: Why There is an Emphasis on the Father's Role; Do the First Five Years of Life Set the Personality Pattern? Why is Cuddling Considered So Important? What to Do When a Child Identifies with the Wrong Sex Parent; Problems of Masturbation and Curiosity Parties. Chapter 11 deals with school age children, and includes topics such as Lewd Stories and Words Brought Home from School, Fear Engendered by Contact with Sex Deviates, Film Showing at School, Explanation of Necking and Petting for Maturing Children, Early Couple Dating of Children is Unnatural.

Wilson W. Grant, M.D., *From Parent to Child About Sex,* (Zondervan, 1975) 183 pages. This excellent Christian book discusses myths, morality, the beginnings of sex education, and then in part 4 explores the growth process from infancy to adulthood, one chapter at a time. It gives specific help in developing sex education at each age level. It contains chapters on the church and the school as they relate to sex education. At the back of the book, there is a 17-page glossary of terms relating to sex education from a medical point of view. To quote from page 12, "Most materials dealing with sex education take the plumbing approach—emphasizing the physical and anatomical aspect of sexual development.

"This book tries to look at sexuality as a whole. While not ignoring the plumbing, it is intended to help parents, particularly Christian parents, understand the more complex and important aspect of sex education—that of attitude and philosophy. The moral issues will be dealt with frankly. Practical ways of dealing with sexuality at each stage of the child's development will be discussed."

Peter Mayle, *Where Did I Come From?* (Tenafly, N.J. Stewart Publications, Inc., 1973) 46 pages. This little book was written to give the facts of life without any nonsense, and with illustrations for young children. The pages, the print, and the illustrations are large for viewing by young children and young school age children. The descriptions and illustrations are frank and accurate. I have found it an excellent tool for sex education in our family.

M.K. Frey, *I Wonder, I Wonder,* (St. Louis: Concordia Publishing House, 1967)

D.Z. Mielach, *A Doctor Talks to Five to Eight Year Olds* (Chicago: Budlong Press, 1974)

R.S. Hummel, *Wonderfully Made* (Concordia, 1967)

Marion O. Lerrigo and Michael A. Cassidy, *A Doctor Talks to Nine to Twelve Year Olds* (Budlong Press, 1974)

Chapters 8 and 9
Tim Stafford, *A Love Story,* (Zondervan, 1977) 160 pages. This is my favorite book relating to sexuality written to teens. In it Stafford covers such questions as "Why Wait?" "Pressure, How Far Do We Go?" "Masturbation," "Singleness," "Homosexuality," "Going Out," and other topics. Stafford is the senior editor of Campus Life Magazine and understands teenagers, their questions and their problems. To quote Stafford on page 13, "Some of us get

to thinking that we are pretty liberated about sex. We learn how to use it effectively, or at least we think we do. But not one of us has a sufficiently wild imagination to have thought it up.

"After all God could have let us reproduce as plants do . . .

"God thought our kind of sex would be more worthwhile. That's why He made us as He did.

"That brings us again to the point of this book. It's not to tell you what you shouldn't do.

"It's not to keep you from fun.

"It's to open you to the freedom of passionate, loving sex in the best way possible."

Norman Wright and Marvin Inmon, *Preparing Youth for Dating, Courtship and Marriage,* (Harvest House, 1978) 69 pages including 12 overhead transparencies and 4 duplication masters. Norman Wright and Marvin Inmon, *A Guidebook to Dating, Waiting, and Choosing a Mate,* (Harvest House, 1978) 158 pages. This teaching material is designed for use by teachers in churches but could also be used by parents in their own preparation of their youth for dating, courtship, and marriage.

These books make an excellent curriculum for family discussions during the teenage years for preparation for dating, courtship, and marriage. The teacher's book includes lecture material and Bible study material along with many learning and discussion activities designed to make learning individual and practical.

Letha Scanzoni, *Sex and the Single Eye,* (Zondervan, 1968) 142 pages. The goal of this book is to encourage each reader to face serious questions. What does it really mean to live for Jesus Christ? And what does being a Christian have to do with one's sex life? The author examines her subject as much as possible in the way that contemporary college students are wondering about it, somewhat in the spirit of an earnest quest. This is an excellent book for college students or older teens.

Helen E. Terkelsen, *Counseling the Unwed Mother,* (Philadelphia: Fortress Press, 1967) 144 pages. This book is part of a pastoral counseling series and deals with unwed motherhood from that perspective. Some of its chapters are: attitudes toward out of wedlock pregnancy, the background and dynamics of the unwed mother and chapters on the counseling process itself. Although this book is written to the pastoral counselor, much of its content would be helpful to a parent whose teenager is an unwed mother and who will not avail herself of pastoral counseling.

Robert R. Wilson, Ed., *Problem of Pregnancy and Abortion Counseling,* (Family Life Publications, Box 427, Saluda, N.C., 1973) 121 pages. Another book written to counselors, this one is authored by several noted writers. It is secular in perspective, and would be helpful in counseling a teenager who is pregnant or one who has gone through an abortion.

A.J. Bueltmann, *Take the High Road* (Concordia, 1967)

Eric W. Johnson, *Love and Sex in Plain Language,* (Philadelphia: J.B. Lippincott Co., 1974)

Evelyn M. Duvall, *Love and the Facts of Life* (New York: Association Press, 1967)

Richard F. Hettlinger, *Living With Sex: The Student's Dilemma* (New York: Seabury Press, Inc., 1966)

Chapter 10

H. Norman Wright, *Premarital Counseling,* (Chicago: Moody Press, 1977) 215 pages. This is a textbook for pastors and counselors on premarital counseling. It gives guidelines for conducting a four-to-six-session premarital counseling program, suggests ways to deal with couples who do not want to be counseled, and recommends ways to deal tactfully with a Christian and a non-Christian who want to marry. Topics that need to be discussed by every engaged couple—in-laws, finances, spiritual life, sex, and more are included. There is a chapter on group premarital counseling and preparation for the church. This book is a must for every church library and would be helpful for parents to have in home libraries as well.

Wes Roberts and H. Norman Wright, *Before You Say I Do,* (Harvest House, 1978) 80 pages. This is a creative resource for premarital preparation and enrichment and can be used as an ideal companion to the cassette series, "Before You Say I do," also by the same authors. It is a study manual designed to assist a young couple as they prepare for marriage. Couples committed to making their marriage a fulfilling and growing relationship will find a wealth of practical ideas for building a firm foundation for their future together. It is designed for a couple to work through together and would be an excellent homework companion to the conversations suggested in chapter 10 of this book.

Chapter 11

Brenda Maddox, *The Half Parent,* (New York: M. Evans and Co., Inc., 1976) 196 pages. This is a very helpful secular book dealing with problems in living with other people's children. Some of the chapter titles are, "Something Like A Witch," "More Than Kin," "The Desolate Stepchild," "Problems of Stepparents," "Incest," "New Babies or No Babies," "Myths and Roles," "Rights and Duties of Stepparents," and "Facing Up to Remarriage." To quote from page 91, "Sexual attraction between stepparents and stepchildren can be a major complication in step families. . . . The real reason why sex becomes an issue is that the incest taboo, the organizing principle of family life, is missing. Nobody in a stepfamily knows what the ground rules are. . . . More than ordinary families, they (stepfamilies) are plagued with flirtations, jealousies, fantasies, and arguments, as well as the physical revulsion that some stepparents complain about." Maddox deals head-on with many of the issues of remarriage and stepparenting. Although it contains no chapter on sex education in the stepfamily, it does include many ideas for improving communication and relationships so that sex education can take place in a much more normal way than otherwise happens in many stepfamilies.